LOWELL THOMAS,
Adventurer

Other Books in the Men of Achievement Series

J. Edgar Hoover, Modern Knight Errant

John Foster Dulles, Peacemaker

Bob Mathias, Champion of Champions

Charles F. Kettering, Inventor and Idealist

Herbert Hoover, Humanitarian

Carl Sandburg, Poet and Patriot

William L. McKnight, Industrialist

J. C. Penney, Merchant Prince

Dr. Albert Schweitzer, Medical Missionary

Ernest Hemingway, Man of Courage

Dr. Frank H. Krusen, Pioneer in Physical Medicine

Nathaniel Leverone, Pioneer in
Automatic Merchandising

Harry A. Bullis, Champion American

Conrad N. Hilton, Hotelier

Lyndon Baines Johnson, Man of Reason

Dr. Norman Vincent Peale, Christian Crusader

Edgar James Helms, the Goodwill Man

General Carlos P. Romulo, Defender of Freedom

Men of Achievement Series

LOWELL THOMAS,
Adventurer

by

MILDRED HOUGHTON COMFORT

Publishers

T. S. DENISON & COMPANY, INC.

Minneapolis

First Printing, February 1965
Second Printing, May 1965
Third Printing, January 1966
Fourth Printing, June 1966
Fifth Printing, February 1967
Sixth Printing, September 1967
Seventh Printing, February 1968
Eighth Printing, July 1968

Printed in the U. S. A.
By THE BRINGS PRESS

Library of Congress Catalog Card Number: 63-14387

DEDICATION

To Adventurers the World Over,
Inventors, Explorers, and Idea Seekers,
for their Discoveries make the World
Better, more Interesting and Wholly
Enjoyable.

"Lives of great men all remind us
We can make our lives sublime,
And departing, leave behind us
Footprints on the sands of time."

—Longfellow

CONTENTS

Chapter One
Cripple Creek Gold 9

Chapter Two
The World of Books 20

Chapter Three
Romance and Army Strategy 29

Chapter Four
Lawrence of Arabia 40

Chapter Five
The Long Career Begins 49

Chapter Six
So Long Until Tomorrow 64

Chapter Seven
Cinerama and the Parthenon 79

Chapter Eight
In the Eternal City 89

Chapter Nine
A Missionary and a Dancer 99

Chapter Ten
The Holy Land 105

Chapter Eleven
The Land of the Pyramids and the Sphinx 111

Chapter Twelve
Land of Gold, Frankincense and Myrrh 117

Chapter Thirteen
A Deep Dam in the Land of Frankincense 124

Chapter Fourteen
The Skyscraper Cities of the Desert 130

Chapter Fifteen
The Rich Oil Men of the Desert 136

Chapter Sixteen
Mount Everest and the Darjeeling Railroad 144

Chapter Seventeen
The Great Wall of China 151

Chapter Eighteen
Memories That Bless and Burn 157

Chapter Nineteen
Into Tibet's Forbidden City 168

Chapter Twenty
Return From Tibet 179

Chapter Twenty-one
A Challenge Too Great to Miss—the
South Pole and the Mount Hagen Area 188

Chapter Twenty-two
The Fabulous Fireplace 204

Chapter Twenty-three
Hammersley Hill 213

Chapter Twenty-four
Lowell Thomas at Home 223

Chapter One

Cripple Creek Gold

A gold miner is an adventurer. He is not trying to get rich, or at any rate that's only part of it, for with the same effort, he could become rich with less labor. Instead he follows the yellow metal for the excitement that the discovery affords him. He braves dangers, sometimes lives in want, and often what he does attain in worldly goods, he squanders. Hope is his star. With a singleness of purpose it holds him to his task. The pick and shovel form the coat of arms for this breed of men. But all who go into gold mining country do not seek gold; they seek to do service in the exciting atmosphere. And these men are adventurers too. Such an adventurer was Dr. Harry Thomas, Lowell Thomas' father.

Gold rushes happen because most men are dreamers. Bob Womack, who first discovered rich, gold-bearing quartz on the cattle ranch where he worked, had visions, or maybe just vision, or maybe he was a cowboy who was just plain lucky—for a while. True he could not foresee that this particular cow pasture would some day net five hundred million dollars in gold. But he dug so many holes looking for this treasure that he was reprimanded by his boss. Cattle were always in danger. In fact, Cripple Creek is said to have derived its name from the cattle that were crippled there, stepping into the uneven creek bed and into the holes nearby dug by young Womack.

Staking out a claim that he called El Paso, the cowboy assured himself that he had discovered gold. Then he sold his El Paso for $500, got drunk and lived to see the mine produce five millions in gold. He died impoverished in Colorado Springs, a ward of kind friends. There were many more like him, men who found gold but did not hold it.

With the news of the discovery of gold, towns mushroomed, and two of them, Cripple Creek and Victor, became famous almost overnight. In altitude both were above 9,000 feet high, surrounded by higher mountains, including Pikes Peak, with Cripple Creek overshadowed by the nearly sharp, regular cone of Mount Pisgah, at an elevation of 10,400 feet, and Victor, "the city of mines," nestled between five mountains, Straub, Bull, Nipple, Battle and Squaw, bristling with the stacks and gallous frames of big and little mines, and terraced with great glistening clumps of granite, quartz, trachite and phonolite. Here was high, healthy country that in latter years was to attract many for the climate alone; air full of ozone, with a real bite in it all year round.

The population increased from a scattered few to over seventy thousand. When gold began to pour down from the hills, the magical building began. Crude houses and tents were replaced by fine homes. Here were also the ubiquitous saloons and bawdy houses, side by side with outfitters who sold everything from mining tools to bacon, flour, tobacco and yard goods. One of America's great department stores got its start here—The May Co.

As wealth increased, gambling became common. Lines formed outside hotels and rooming houses. Restaurants at meal hours were overcrowded. Finding a house to buy or a room to rent was soon as difficult as to find an unstaked claim. Houses were seldom locked. A woman could walk anywhere at any time of day or night unmolested. Dwellings were not so sacred. A miner, returning from work, might find his shack appropriated or even moved away.

Twice fire destroyed most of the booming gold camp but it was rebuilt with stone and brick. By the year of 1900 there were in the Cripple Creek district forty-one assay offices, ninety-one lawyers, forty-six brokerages, eighty-eight doctors and dentists, fourteen newspapers, seventy saloons, and, as one resident expressed it, one very busy coroner.

Here Texas Guinan launched her entertainment career as a church organist; Jack Dempsey worked as a mucker in the mines, and Jack Johnson and Tex Rickard as saloon men. Here Lowell Thomas carved his initials on schoolroom desks, first at the Garfield and later at Victor "High," just next door to the Red Light District—the "Cribs."

Who was this Lowell Thomas who was destined to become world famous, who was to travel millions and millions of miles, visit nearly every part of the known and the almost unknown world, who was to report events over a lifetime and to be heard by more people than anyone in the world? Cripple Creek-Victor people said he was a chap who was lucky in his choice of parents. The boy was brought up right!

The man whose mellifluous voice saying nightly, "Good evening, everybody," and ending a broadcast with "So long until tomorrow" is known everywhere from radio, TV, motion pictures and his books, by his full name, Lowell Thomas. A few called him, affectionately, Tommy. He was born in Darke County, Ohio, in a village called Woodington, today known as the birthplace of two widely different personalities, Lowell Thomas and Annie Oakley, Miss Sure Shot of the Buffalo Bill circus.

The boy's birth was recorded as Lowell Jackson Thomas, and the date as April 6, 1892. The Jackson for a great-grandfather who lived among the Indians. He was a sturdy eight-year-old when he came with his parents to live in the Cripple Creek gold mining district of Colorado.

He was the product of many generations of forebears on both sides of the family who came to America early. The Thomas family was of English background, perhaps from the hills of Wales in pre-Roman days. Grandmother Thomas, whose maiden name was Jackson, settled in Martha's Vineyard, and others, in a spirit of courage and adventure, joined her. The Thropes and Wycoffs arrived from Holland during the period of Peter Stuyvesant, and the Wagners, who were English, also of pre-revolutionary days, pushed west from

Pennsylvania and accepted payment in lands. Grandfather Wagner settled in Ohio, and, still restless, moved on with the Parkmans to Oregon as part of a covered wagon train. Our modern troubadour's father, Harry George Thomas, was named after Lighthorse Harry Lee, and General George H. Thomas of Chickamauga fame. He, too, was a magnificent reconteur, telling many a tale of the settling of the frontier as he witnessed it.

Lowell's parents were well-educated, well-adjusted people—their education far beyond the average schooling of their day. Both were teachers, and the maternal grandmother was not only a writer for the local paper, but a poet as well. The family was the first in the community to go away to college. Before deciding to become a physician the father specialized in science, intending to teach geology, botany, and astronomy, subjects that became his lifelong hobbies and which he passed on to his son.

"H. G." never had intended to make mining his life's work, nor did he seek riches. He moved his family on west from Iowa to Colorado when Lowell was eight years old because going west was the thing to do—he had worked there between semesters when at college — and in Cripple Creek he already had an older brother, a mining engineer.

How the doctor managed to get his fine medical education is a story in itself. He married while still in medical school, and the young couple had a baby to care for. He worked summers, would teach for a year and then go on.

He started the practice of medicine in Kirkman,

Iowa, where other relatives had settled in the tall corn country. It was a typical country practice. Whenever he got a few hundred dollars ahead, he would go back to Chicago to study. He also managed a few courses and another degree at the University of Nebraska. Not only was he a physician, he was a scholar as well. His curiosity was insatiable.

While in western Iowa, his brother, the mining engineer, wrote of the big boom in Cripple Creek. Cory Thomas had no problem to persuade the young doctor to come out, for Dr. Harry already was enamoured of the high country and the challenge of frontier life.

Immediately he moved his family to the Rockies, to the Cripple Creek District, that is to the lively mining center just over the hill at Victor. It was here that Pherbia, Lowell's sister, was born.

In a way it was more than a rough-and-ready mining town for them; for they lived above the sordid. In this isolated, volcanic area, life could be even more wholesome than strangers might expect of a mining camp. The gold mines paid good wages, and many of the workers were students working to get money for college. Because there was money in practically every pocket, there was no thieving. The amazing opera house they built brought the finest talent from all over the world. Lowell and Pherbia enjoyed great Shakespearean actors, singers of distinction, and fine lecturers. On their transcontinental swing, everybody from Jenny Lind to Joseph Jefferson, John Drew and Lillian Russell visited "The world's greatest gold camp." They were constantly stimulated.

The doctor had the finest library in The District,

over three thousand volumes. No field of interest had escaped his interest, and, in his spare time, he shared his knowledge with his children. Early in life Lowell was reading from such classics as Boswell's "Life of Jonson," "Pilgrim's Progress," Milton's "Paradise Lost," Dante's "Inferno," Scott, Dickens, Kipling, Emerson, Lowell, Hawthorne, and above all, a fat edition of "The Arabian Nights," all from the family bookshelves. The Thomas household never had much money, for the good doctor was more interested in serving than in collecting bills, but there was always money for books. Besides, there were riches in earth and sky, free for the knowing. His interest in astronomy never waned. Often on a clear, cold night, he would take the children on a climb to point out the planets and the galaxies of stars. He would point out Orion, Arcturus, and the Pleiades, and the Transit of Venus. For the latter heavenly occasion the children joined the next-door neighbor who had a six-inch telescope. From the top of nearby Squaw Mountain the view of the heavens was superb. Every constellation in the sky became a familiar skymark. Walking home from the evening church services, the father would point into the heavens and ask, "What star is that up there, almost obscured by the clouds?"

If they hesitated, he would say, "You should be able to tell by the position in the sky, in spite of clouds."

Walking over the hills, the doctor would pick up a rock, break it with his geologist's hammer and expect the children to know the mineral content. Then he taught them geology and stimulated their interest, not only in the sparkling heavens but in the earth under the firmament. The world of trees and flowers was theirs too, the columbines, the Iceland poppies, and the wild rose.

The mother did all her own housework, laundry, cooking, and sewing, yet she made time to help out in the Methodist church which the family attended, and never failed in civic projects in which all took part.

She loved the new country and, in the fall when the aspens were gold along the creeks or shone against the spruce, she spent joyous hours with her children gathering wild grapes or buffalo berries for winter jams. She sang in the choir and cooked for the church suppers.

The house never lacked flowers, from early spring when the first short-stemmed, furry crocuses appeared in a soup plate on the dining room table to the anemones, the columbine, and the flaming paintbrush against the gray sage. Pherbia arranged bouquets for every occasion, from a supper party to a wedding.

Oftentimes the doctor's fees came in the form of vegetables or logs or game. He might even be given a kitten or a puppy.

Since there were ninety-six trains a day on three "lines," "The Midland," "The Short Line," and "The Florence and Cripple Creek," carrying gold ore to Colorado Springs, there was little attention to road making or conditioning. The doctor often made his way through deep snow when it was too high even to manage on horseback. He never failed his patients.

He was never too weary to read aloud or to hear his children recite their pieces. His own father had

Lowell Thomas at Cripple Creek during his gold-mining days.

Lowell Thomas begins radio broadcasting.

Lowell Thomas and Lowell Thomas, Jr., age 8, on their farm in Dutchess County.

been a teacher, and elocution was in his very blood. Whenever Lowell had an assignment that involved speaking, and he soon was much in demand, the doctor would take his son to the Opera House or the Masonic Temple for a rehearsal. There he would train him to speak for an audience. Lowell would be instructed to speak loudly, clearly, and to throw his voice, aspirate his h's, and never drop the ends of sentences. Any flaw in pronunciation was corrected. If the doctor could hear him today, pronouncing correctly all the different foreign words he needs to know in his broadcasting, he would be indeed proud. In fact, he did hear him for the first fifteen of his thirty-five years "on the air."

The young boy says he didn't altogether appreciate his father's instruction. But in only one area did he balk—he refused to use the elaborate gestures that were the style for professional elocutionists. So it was that it became natural for Lowell to gravitate to public speaking, though at the time he could not even dream that his was to become the most famous speaking voice in the world, a voice that would be familiar to millions right around the globe.

In his father, Lowell had an example of scholarliness. There was somehow money for books and fine entertainment. Any money saved went into search for further knowledge.

By 1914 the busy doctor had acquired enough savings once again to continue his medical studies. He had always wanted to study at the University of Vienna, but his plans miscarried. First he went east, to Johns Hopkins for a summer of work, and then he met Sir William Osler who changed his life's course.

The wartime need in England for doctors was desperate, and in response to this the young mining surgeon went to England to become a member of the Osler staff at the First London Hospital. He served in England and Italy, until America entered the war, and finally came home as a colonel in Pershing's army, plus two years as a full professor at the great American University at Beirut, in the Near East.

Back in the United States he again set up practice, this time in the East. And when he was in his eighties, he went back to Victor for a visit.

"Old Doc has come to town!" The news flew from door to door. "Old Doc is back!"

Old patients came flocking to see their beloved physician and surgeon . . . "Remember, Doc, how you set my broken leg in that mine shaft? Good as new. . . . I'll pull up my pants and show you the clean scar!" . . . "See this scar, Doc? Hadn't been for you, I wouldn't be here to say 'Welcome home' now." . . . A shy woman speaks, saying, "I'm Viola, Doc. Remember me?"

He did remember. "Yes, Viola," he said in that kindly voice so familiar to the people of Victor. "I delivered you in a mining shack in the dead of winter. You were premature as I guess your mother told you, and I made you an incubator—used blankets and whiskey bottles filled with hot water."

The people crowded about their doctor. The famous son, Lowell Thomas, was there to take part in the festivities, but he stood back and watched with delight the encomiums heaped upon his father. This man who had healed and helped these people had given much to his own family too. He had given his son training, courage, and an incentive to learn.

It was good to see the old family home, and especially that notation on the ell porch that read:

> THIS WAS THE BOYHOOD HOME OF LOWELL J. THOMAS, A GRADUATE OF THE VICTOR HIGH SCHOOL OF 1910, AND LATER FAMOUS AS NEWSCASTER, AUTHOR AND WORLD EXPLORER. HE IS THE SON OF DR. AND MRS. HARRY THOMAS, FOR MANY YEARS ACTIVE AND RESPECTED CITIZENS OF VICTOR.

How his eyes must have misted as an oldtimer said, "Wal, Doc, you sure got that boy of yours off on the right foot." But by now the son also had been to eastern universities and off to war, and the family now settled in the East, at Princeton and finally on the "Jersey Coast."

Chapter Two

The World of Books

One small boy in Victor, Colorado, having been brought up in a household that boasted of little money but much reading, proved to be an exceptional pupil. His high school teacher, Mabel Barbee, who years later became the famous authoress Mabel Barbee Lee, confessed that one sophomore lad in particular loomed as a continuous challenge to her meager knowledge of modern history. His interests extended from Alaska to Angola, from Persia to Peru, from Iceland to India. He not only was fascinated by the tales of strange places the gold miners had been, there were all the strange lands he had read about. He was quiet-mannered and fine-looking, with dark wavy hair and bright, serious eyes. The name of the brilliant student was Lowell Thomas.

He was the son of Dr. Harry Thomas, city physician, and one of the intellectual leaders of the town. The mother, in spite of her erudition, devoted her spare time to church and club work. The doctor, in his spare hours, shared his vast knowledge with Lowell and Pherbia, Lowell's young sister.

No field of study had escaped the father's wide-ranging curiosity, and some of this desire for knowing things he passed on to his son. And like the son, he was to know all sorts and conditions of men. Not only was he to enjoy the cultured people of the gold towns, but the seamy side as well. Mining camp activities were often vicious, with stabbings and murders, and in the mines there were endless accidents, premature explosions, men crushed by falling rock.

Victor also had its tenderloin district which boys and girls had to pass going and coming from high school. A slight effort seemed to have been made to hide it from view by that handsome, red-brick theater, THE GRAND OPERA HOUSE, which towered above and overshadowed "The Row." It failed that purpose, but the well-equipped, well-appointed theater did become a center for both amusement and culture. Its entertainments were part of the children's education. The gold miners and their families loved entertainment, and most families owned pianos. The sounds of scales being practiced after school hours and on Saturdays echoed up and down the treeless streets. But early settlers found it hard to get used to long-haired musicians, especially violinists. A violin, a fiddle, was still regarded as the instrument for hillbilly tunes, like "Turkey in the Straw," and "Old Dan Tucker"—and always "The Irish Washerwoman."

Being a gold camp, Victor had the reputation of being a free spending, rather wild community. Actually, it was a center of culture in many ways. The children did find "books in the running brooks," brooks that all cascaded fast down the mountains, but they also found it in their libraries, and the handsome theater. The town welcomed Sousa's Band, Primrose and Dockstader's Minstrels, Max Figman in "The Man on the Box" and Olga Nethersole in her shocker, "Sappho." They heard Ellen Beach Yaw "with a range of nearly four octaves."

Of the arrival of Fritzi Scheff in "Mlle. Modiste," touring with her own fifteen-piece orchestra, the teacher tells a tender story.

One violin teacher, Professor Hans Albert, was considered the town character, walking bareheaded down the main street, his long, unruly reddish hair blowing in the wind, his frock coat much too long for him. His short mustache was always carefully clipped and he wore an air of assurance. The story was that he had once been famous in Vienna, and that he had come to the high Rockies for his asthma. It was hard to believe that he had been a protege of Emperor Franz Joseph at the age of nine, that his teacher was no less a personality than Swedermann, the renowned maestro at the Royal Conservatory in Wurzburg. It was even harder to believe that when he was only sixteen, his Majesty the Emperor appointed him Konzertmeister with the Imperial Opera. . . . Three years later, the Professor revealed, he was called to America to become first violinist with the renowned Theodore Thomas Symphony Orchestra of Chicago and was invited by President and Mrs. Grover Cleveland to give a recital at the White House. . . . Now he was a sick, tired, and lonely old man striving to earn enough to send for his fiancee.

When Hans Albert learned that Fritzi Scheff's conductor had suffered a mild heart attack in the high altitude and had to be sent down to a hospital in Denver, he offered to substitute.

From Marbel Barbee Lee we get the story of that dramatic evening. The atmosphere was tense in the Grand Opera House. Would the local genius embarrass or even fail his townspeople? But the moment Hans Albert tapped the music stand with his baton and nodded to the musicians, the audience burst into applause, forcing him to bow grandly before signaling the start of the overture. He seemed to be lifted into another world, a world he had known well and loved so long ago.

As the velvet curtains parted and the chorus held the final note for the entrance of M'lle. Modiste, Fritzi Scheff floated lightly down the stage in her blue satin gown and silver slippers, her golden curls brushed atop her head.

At the cue for her famous ballad, "Kiss Me Again," pride seemed to flow from the delicate fingers of the maestro to the baton, as if he were aware that he and the lovely lady shared the same mother tongue and had been nourished by the same musical traditions.

When she sang the finale and melted into her lover's arms, the theater was suddenly plunged into unplanned darkness. But out of the inky blackness came the quieting strains of violin music. The audience was charmed into listening until the lights came on again.

After her last bow, Fritzi Scheff thanked the people for her reception. Then looking down at Hans Albert, she added, "I would like especially to thank your gifted maestro for showing such presence of mind in averting what might have been a disaster." She reached down and grasped his hand, saying, "You are a true artist . . . danke schoen . . . Auf Wiedersehen!"

Such an incident could not have happened in the average community. Even though the Cripple Creek district was a roaring mining camp, it was also a Western city where perhaps a million people were lured in search of El Dorado. Many students who came out from the East to work in the mines in order to earn their college degrees left their names on the history records of Cripple Creek.

Today two names of widely different attainment stand out. Jack Dempsey, sportsman and prize fighter, once a mucker at the Portland mine where young Lowell worked as a "trammer, ore-sorter and assayer!" Jack went on to win the world's heavyweight championship, acclaimed by many as the greatest of the world's pugilists; the first fighter ever to draw a million-dollar gate.

Bernard Baruch, just out of college, had roughed it in some of Battle Mountain's mines, and even battled with his fists on one of the "lower levels." He returned East to make his mark as a financier, pundit, and counselor to the nation's Presidents.

But the sky of Victor was arched with rainbows

when Dr. Harry Thomas came back to Victor in his old age to see his home preserved.

Quite a few of the people had kept track of the fine doctor's accomplishments, especially those who had had the benefit of his surgical skill. In his seventies he was still practicing medicine in Asbury Park, New Jersey, and had handled medical and surgical problems for an immense naval project.

Lowell followed in his father's footsteps when it came to acquiring formal knowledge. He went in for schooling on a large scale, securing degrees from Valparaiso University, the University of Denver, Kent College of Law in Chicago, and Princeton University.

"I went to Valparaiso University in northern Indiana because I could work my way," he explained. "Moreover, it might be added, the scholastic standards were high; Valparaiso, with a student body in those days about the same as the ancient University at Boston, was referred to as 'the poor man's Harvard.' "

He was just out of high school when he enrolled at the university in both the freshman and sophomore classes. Some weeks later when Professor Kinsey, the vice president, called him into his office to inform him that double registration was against the rules, he pleaded to be allowed to carry out the program he had set for himself, until he failed.

He did not fail. Instead, he finished the four-year course in two years and secured both his bachelor's and master's degrees.

A college education, however, he found was not a

guarantee of a job. He went back to the pick and shovel in a gold mine, this time "The Empire State" at Altman, "highest incorporated town in the world." As time went on, his father sent him money when he was away at school; but he himself was forever getting jobs to earn more. Nor was he fussy about jobs. He had been a gold miner and a cowpuncher as well. He had sold newspapers in the gambling halls and saloons of Victor and Cripple Creek. At college he cared for furnaces, acted as a cook and waiter, even as a valet to a cow for a professor. He sold real estate, lectured, taught, worked as a reporter. As a teen-ager, when working in the mines, somebody asked him why he worked when obviously his family could afford to take care of his expenses.

"Everybody works out here," he explained.

In the Cripple Creek District when he went to Sunday school, which he always did, he says he was fascinated by the music of the organist, Texas Guinan. Texas was a natural entertainer, as popular in Sunday school as in New York later when she became a celebrity with her speakeasy greeting, "Hello, Sucker."

Lowell found work on The Victor Record and gave the newspaper his all, stimulated by a rivalry with Ralph Carr who later became governor of Colorado. The red-hot competition proved invaluable to both and they were lifelong pals—after they went on to wider fields, one in law and politics, the other as a modern Marco Polo.

More education was always his goal. While working later on a newspaper in Denver, he did graduate work at the University of Denver and added two more degrees.

Then east again, this time to Chicago, where he enrolled at the Chicago Kent College of Law to study law at night. Here at Kent, he was given a place on the faculty, and for two years, he was in charge of the Department of Forensic Oratory and at the same time filled a full-time job on a Chicago daily newspaper. In his second year he was offered a job with the then largest law firm in America, Winston, Payne, Strawn and Shaw.

Instead, he went east to Princeton to work for a doctor's degree, and there also was invited to join the faculty. He proved a great teacher, admired and loved by the students. But his primary talent, his friends judged, was his special eye and ear for news. Even in the simplest story he saw the unusual, the significant. Moreover, he had the ability to tell a story so it interested the general public.

Of his Princeton days Dean Hugh Scott Taylor, now Sir Hugh, who had been a classmate, remembered that Lowell Thomas knew everybody and never had to ask a name twice. Sir Hugh said, "He had a voracious appetite for getting to know people and still does. That's part of his skill."

His neatness and taste were never confined to choice of words but spilled over into a sort of sartorial splendor. Novelist Homer Croy's report of his first meeting with Lowell Thomas is honest and amusing. He says, "The first time I saw Lowell was at the Players Club in New York during his years of teaching and studying at Princeton. I shall never forget the sight. He was wearing a tall, stiff, single-ply collar, an ascot tie with a pearl stickpin, a long-tailed Prince Albert coat with two cloth-covered buttons in the small of the back, and a vest with white piping. He also had on striped pants that only an American ambassador is brave enough to be seen in. I sat in awe!" Lowell Thomas denies he ever wore such an outfit except at a wedding. He's still an impressive dresser, but has long since given up the piping and the cloth-covered buttons. Even in London, Paris, or maybe in Hong Kong, he is a marked man because of his Colorado "Stetson," and other things that remind him of his boyhood in the Rockies.

The preciseness of his grooming has stood him in good stead with all the traveling he was to do. He has always packed a bag neatly, with a place for everything and everything in its place.

His first travels, fired by the stories of far-flung places he had heard in the mining camps of Cripple Creek, began with two summer expeditions to Alaska. These were to be the first of many journeys.

Chapter Three

Romance and Army Strategy

One of Lowell Thomas' secretaries once said, "I've never known him to take NO for an answer."

That might have been true in the world of business, but in the realm of romance, he was what we call a "Rejected Romeo."

There was only one girl in the world for him, and he proposed marriage to her by letter. With his gift for clarity of expression, he should have been able to compose a love letter that a girl would place among her souvenirs of rose petals and cherish forever. Frances Ryan said NO. She was not interested.

The story is told of a roommate dropping in on him in Chicago and recalling the days when they had been at the University of Denver. When the conversation got around to girls, the friend asked, "Which girl did you like best?"

The Lowell Thomas reply was "Oh, Fran Ryan was the loveliest girl I've ever known."

"Did you tell her so?" his old friend inquired.

"No," young Thomas admitted, "but I will."

She had been a freshman when he was a senior, and she stood out among all the other girls for beauty, brains and charm. Her hair was full of golden lights and her eyes were bluer than the Colorado sky, and she was trim as a young aspen. She was Scotch-Irish, and French. That is, her father, Harry Ryan, was Irish and French, and her mother, Eunice MacCorkle, was a Scot, both of pioneer stock. Her grandfather Ryan had been in the Revolutionary War and after the war, had gone west in a covered wagon to settle in Nebraska, having received land in payment for his services as a soldier of General Washington.

Like many of his neighbors, Harry Ryan had pulled himself up by his bootstraps to a post with the traffic department of the Burlington, on the run between Montana, Denver and Chicago.

Frances was born in Hot Springs, South Dakota, but when she was nine months old the family moved to Billings, Montana, then later settled in Colorado.

To earn her way through college, Frances worked in the registrar's office and later taught in a country school. In those days the teacher not only instructed her pupils in all the subjects of various grades, but built the fires, swept out the schoolhouse, and even handled a team of horses.

She knew Lowell Thomas as a prominent senior, who was also doing graduate work, and editor of "The Clarion," the university paper. Unlike the girls who flocked about him, she was not especially impressed. At least she told herself she wasn't. Besides, beaux were many. She was surrounded by old friends and schoolmates. To her, Lowell Thomas seemed a sort of dandy—the dude from Cripple Creek with his high, stiff collar that almost choked him, and his western hat. There was a foursome that often went about together, but Lowell was the partner of the other girl.

When the proposal of marriage by letter came, she was vexed rather than flattered. There was an assurance that she read between the lines that was irritating. She simply said NO and no question about it.

In the meantime, Lowell Thomas was not dismayed and he certainly had no intention of giving her up. He would work out his salvation in person. That's what he should have done in the first place, he reasoned. Simply to get to Denver and do this, he managed to get a job writing about the coming World's Fair in San Francisco. On the way he, of course, stopped off to see Fran in Denver. This time he proposed in person—only to be turned down again.

"Why, you didn't even date me when you were in college," she reminded him.

She watched him leave, apparently accepting defeat. But he was to return as she might have known he would. All the time he was on the West Coast and in Alaska, he thought of her and his determination never faltered.

Entering Princeton in 1914 to study constitutional law, he spent week ends showing his Alaskan films and appearing before eastern audiences, women's clubs and other groups. Realizing that this was more remunerative than teaching, he set off for Alaska again the following summer for more material. He received no answers to the letters he had been writing Frances Ryan, so he stopped off once more in Colorado, then went on to Alaska again, and this time home via the Grand Canyon. Fran was still adamant.

The start of World War I was destined to make a change in many lives and it did in theirs. To begin with, the war made European travel impossible. Why not see America first? That was a new slogan, proposed by Franklin K. Lane, secretary of the Interior. He heard about Lowell Thomas and his account of his travels in Alaska, sent for him and asked him to lead a "See America First" campaign. But by the time Lowell had resigned from Princeton, we were in the war, whereupon Secretary Lane came up with another idea. He proposed that the young man from Princeton should hurry over to Europe and gather material on the war, to help arouse America. The only drawback was money. Perhaps a hundred thousand dollars would be needed—and Congress was not yet ready to supply it.

Not wanting to ask for a special appropriation, Secretary Lane put the question to twenty-five-year-old Lowell: "Do you suppose you could raise the hundred thousand?"

It may have been a mere rhetorical question, but Lowell Thomas went to Chicago and put his problem to a famous lawyer, Silas Strawn, whom he had helped on a big legal case, following which his lawyer friend had said, "If there ever is anything we can do for you, just let us know."

Now that's just what he did and in no time at all he had rounded up seventeen multi-millionaires who supplied the money.

From then on events moved fast. They had to. Time was of the essence. Lowell took the train immediately to Denver, his third crossing of the continent to get Frances Ryan to say YES. This time she gave her consent, and they were married on August 4, 1917, in Denver at the Ryan home, in a ceremony performed by Dr. David Lough who had been their professor of philosophy at the university. Frances wore a bridal gown of white tulle over satin and an exquisite veil, and she carried a bouquet of white roses and stephanotis.

Life moved on with dizzying rapidity for them—and has ever since. In no time at all, it seemed, they had secured passports, visas, and were on a transport that landed them at Bordeaux, France. For a honeymoon they made a hurried tour of the country, the rich vineyards, military camps, and were taken to visit the famous sculptor, Bertillon, who had made the model for the Statue of Liberty. They celebrated gayly in Paris and, yet in the midst of all the joyfulness, there was an undercurrent of anxiety as they watched men march to the front lines. To be of real use, Frances joined the Red Cross and was sent to Genoa, Italy, to look after the Venetian lace workers who had all fled from their homes on the canals. She worked there for a year seeing her young husband only when he could pass through Genoa on his way to and from the Italian, the Balkan and the Palestine and Arabian fronts. She says she will always remember the palace, her headquarters, where most of the food was stored. She was given the key and rationed the food on order.

Besides the care of the rationed food, the bride faced the problem of helping the refugees, supervision of the men and women who were vital to the lace-making industry.

It was not long after the battle of the Piave that the bridegroom came to Genoa with the news that he had permission to take his bride to the front lines, provided she could get leave from the Red Cross. The two of them went off in a car and, for the first time since the war had started, Frances saw dead young soldiers on the ground. It was a sorrowful sight and she was so full of pity that her eyes were blinded by tears. But even as she gazed about, bullets whizzed past her. She and her husband were being sniped at. They ran headlong for shelter in a little chapel. The City of Canals was all but deserted. Aside from Italian army and naval personnel, the young Prince of Wales, pink cheeked, shy, but friendly, and his aides were the only others in Venice.

During the war the bridal couple had little time together, Fran busy with the Red Cross, Lowell on his roving war assignment. One night in Venice he saw a military bulletin fastened to the sandbags in front of St. Mark's Cathedral. He read this with special interest. If General Sir Edmund H. H. Allenby were being assigned to the British forces in Egypt, surely something important was about to happen "out East." Soon he was in touch with the British Foreign Office in London and through the famous novelist and statesman, John Buchan, he pulled strings that landed him in Egypt along with Harry Chase, his photographer.

Palestine, to Christians everywhere, had for nineteen centuries been the Holy Land. Christian crusaders a thousand years ago had fought to wrest it from the Moslems, only to fail. The capture of Jerusalem by General Allenby was a military miracle. Not a shot was fired.

Lowell Thomas was in Jerusalem, soon expecting to return to Europe and join the Americans in France, when something unforeseen happened. While bargaining with an Arab merchant over some Damascus silk, he saw a group of tall, dark Bedouins, heavily bearded, in company with a slender young man of fair complexion but also wearing Arab robes and headdress. Curious, he noticed that the young man was blue-eyed and beardless. He followed the group down the street, lost them in the Christian Street crowds, and a bit later dropped in at the headquarters of Sir Ronald Storrs, the governor of the Holy City, to inquire who the fair Arab might be. His reporter's instinct told him there was a story in this man. And what a story it turned out to be! One of the most dramatic of all time!

The governor walked to a door in his office that led to an inner room, and throwing it open, there sat the blond "Arab," whom Sir Ronald introduced to his American guest as Colonel Thomas Edward Lawrence, an ex-British archaeologist, now "The Uncrowned King of Arabia" as Storrs referred to him. This introduction was the beginning of a friendship that brought world fame to both. For Lowell Thomas was the first to tell the world about Lawrence. He is known far and wide as the "discoverer of Lawrence of Arabia."

Lowell Thomas, in the years to come, said that he admired Lawrence more than any human being he had ever met in all his around-the-world adventures. He had heard vaguely about the man before he met him—how he had been rejected by the British army, only to join the British Intelligence Service, and ask to be sent to Arabia. The Turks were threatening the Suez Canal and all of Egypt. Lawrence joined the Arabs, and, dressed in Arab garb, called on Feisal, one of the sons of Hussein, Sherif of Mecca, a leader of the Arab rebels, and won his friendship. Lawrence had long been a student of strategy, and from now on played the key role in the desert war against the Turks.

Young Thomas persuaded Allenby to let him join Lawrence in Arabia. He put on Arab garb himself, and with Harry Chase and his motion picture camera, he headed for the Hedjaz, "Holy Arabia," where the desert campaign was fought.

How valuable all the material he brought back might be, not even Lowell Thomas could dream.

When he finally did return to Europe, the war was soon over. This meant there no longer was any reason to hurry home. Moreover, a revolution had just broken out in Central Europe, and he decided to find out about it. On this, Generals Foch and Pershing were not co-operative. However, he bet fellow correspondent Webb Waldron that he could do what others were trying in vain to do, get them both into Germany. Off they went, and several times failed. Then, one day near the Rhine in Lorraine at the city of Mulhouse, they ran into an American in Red Cross uniform who had an ambulance and was under orders to pick up stragglers coming out of German prison camps. How would he like to drive a couple of stragglers the other way? He would. The two lay down in the ambulance and the driver piled stretchers and blankets over them. In this way they eluded the border guards and after many adventures they were in the midst of the German revolution, the one that caused Kaiser Wilhelm to flee to Holland.

Now followed one of the most exciting periods of his adventurous life.

While on a Berlin roof, Lowell Thomas' motion picture camera was mistaken for a machine gun and he was shot at by the patrols on the street below. Actually, a bullet grazed his side.

One report was that he swam the Rhine and got back to Paris just in time for the Versailles peace conference. Actually, a French cruiser that stopped at Hamburg for fuel, picked them up and took them back to France, where President Wilson heard about them through his advisor, Colonel House, and Lowell Thomas and Webb Waldron made a firsthand report on what was happening inside Germany.

Meanwhile, Fran, who had returned to Denver, and not quite sure what was happening to her still wandering husband, got a great shock.

One day a "Denver Post" reporter called at the Ryan home on Milwaukee Street and broke the news to Fran that her husband had been shot in a Berlin riot. Fortunately, the press dispatch from Germany was inaccurate and within twenty-four hours she had a wire from him saying he had been shot through the hat, not through the heart.

For the next few years they were on the move telling the story of Lawrence of Arabia and of Allenby's campaign in Palestine, to audiences in many lands around the world. This began with a spectacular season in New York, first at the great Century Theatre, and then at Madison Square Garden, where an English impresario signed Lowell up for a London season. Whereupon in the British capital his success was even greater. More than a million people came to hear him and see his films at Covent Garden Royal Opera House and at The Royal Albert Hall. In fact, at the Albert Hall, which seats some eleven thousand, he made the first "run" in the history of that huge auditorium. Although the British were enthralled by his account of their Palestine campaign and the fall of Jerusalem, it was the first time they had ever heard of T. E. Lawrence, whom Lowell Thomas now made a legendary figure, and in so doing made himself famous. For his "show" he created the first "live" prologue ever used with motion pictures. Also with his own narration—delivered in person—he used a sixty-piece orchestra and sound effects, a thing never done before.

The news of what the young American was doing went around the world. Britishers returning home from far-flung outposts of the empire even cabled for seats to hear this Yankee story of the romantic and adventurous deeds of Allenby and Lawrence and their men. Nothing like it had ever happened before or has ever happened since.

His London sensation was followed by the longest personal appearance tour ever made by a public speaker. Australia and New Zealand came next. Then audiences in Ceylon, India, Burma, Malaya and on around the globe, finally ending with a three-year tour of most of the cities and larger towns of the United States and Canada.

Lowell Thomas still looks back upon this as in some ways the number one adventure of his life—an experience shared with his wife who encouraged, inspired and helped him in endless ways. While he himself was speaking in Dublin, their now famous son was born in a London nursing home. A boat trip across the stormy English Channel had made Fran seasick and she was relieved on landing to be settled in a nursing home on Wigmore Street.

Sonny, as he was to be called for a good many years, even though he was christened Lowell Thomas Junior, was born on October 6, 1923. It is an amusing fact that on his thirty-ninth birthday he called his parents from Alaska to announce that he was no longer SONNY. Henceforth they'd please call him LOWELL.

The Thomases came back to America accompanied by a nine-month-old baby and a Swedish nurse. At first they lived in Asbury Park, New Jersey, and then in 1926 they moved to Clover Brook Farm in Dutchess County, N. Y., and lived there for nineteen years until moving over the ridge to Hammersley Hill in 1945.

Chapter Four

Lawrence of Arabia

Of Lawrence of Arabia, Lowell Thomas often said that he admired him beyond any other human being he ever met, and that the day he walked along Christian Street in Jerusalem and caught his first glimpse of the White Arab was perhaps the most fortuitous of his life. In his description of the encounter he said, "Walking through the streets of the Holy City, I saw a man, slim and short of stature. I thought he might be a Circassian, perhaps of Sherifian rank. At any rate, he had on what I surmised might be the white silk robes of an Arab prince, and in his sash the short, curved gold sword distinctive of the Ashraf, descendants of the Prophet. But it wasn't his regalia nor his Ashraian insignia that made him a personage to wonder about, it was his bearing.

"When under his Sherifian agal and kuffieh I perceived the blue eyes and Norman English features, I wondered if he could be the reincarnation of a Crusader in the train of Richard."

The story of how the men experienced an instant interest in each other, a liking that developed into a friendship, has often been told. Lowell Thomas was lucky enough to be the only observer allowed to go into the desert with Lawrence and bring back an on-the-scene story of the Arabian revolt which ultimately reached its climax with the fall of Damascus. But the aftermath was hardly less astounding than the desert war and the recording of the story.

Lowell Thomas was destined to make Lawrence of Arabia famous and Lawrence was destined to give Lowell Thomas a start on a career that made him world famous too.

When Lawrence left Damascus after his victories, he was physically exhausted, but he had not lost his zest for Arab independence. To the men of the desert he may have been a King Maker, but Feisal, once safely on his throne, was startled when the man who had placed him there abruptly removed himself from the scene. As for the American chronicler of that story, the Arab revolt stimulated Lowell Thomas' imagination. The desert, with its trackless sands, its rocks and its mirages, made for a subject to stir his heart. As for T. E. Lawrence, he was no ordinary intelligence officer, but a crusader dedicated to a cause. He was, he admitted, an enthusiast concerning everything Arab and Arabian. He prodded the nomads and townspeople to strike against the Turks. He strove, too, to get the tribes to cease their feuds and to work together. What he wanted for them was a free Arabia and a Pan-Arabic Council. Because he himself was a humble person and yet so engaging, the Arab people came to love him with an affection that was close to worship.

Lowell Thomas felt the force of this frail appearing man who possessed such unexpected strength, who could endure pain, weariness, and ill treatment and not let it break his spirit. Later on belittlers accused him of exhibitionism, but Lowell Thomas discovered quite a different man. When they first met in Jerusalem, Lawrence had his own explanation as to why he wore Arabian regalia. He had come across the desert through the Turkish lines which he could not have done in British uniform. To obtain the pictures he needed, Harry Chase, his photographer, related a tale of Lowell Thomas distracting Lawrence with talk about Hittite archaeology while he, Chase, manipulated his camera. Actually, Lawrence was modest but not camera-shy. Not only did he allow himself to be photographed, but he persuaded scores of Bedouin sheiks to let the camera "shoot" them despite the fact that they all believed the camera was an invention of Eblis, or the devil.

It is only human to enjoy fame, and Lawrence may have enjoyed this as nearly all men do. He may even have enjoyed wearing Sherifian regalia. Eventually his association and friendship with Feisal in the desert did indeed make him a king-maker. And, he was a student of military strategy.

His career was, as the world now knows, fantastic. As an Oxford archaeologist he had been working on the excavation of ancient cities in the Near East when the war broke out. In this work he had learned to appreciate the Arabs and resented the tyrannical Turks. Later, as a leader of desert fighters, his ability to demoralize communications and carry out destructive raids was phenomenal. There was a price on his head. To be with him during this desert war gave Lowell Thomas the material for the world tour that brought fame to both. True, he had his report for the government, but after the war ended that was secondary. It was his account of the war in the Near East and his stunning pictorial record that blazed a new trail in the entertainment world. He called the story "With Allenby in Palestine and Lawrence in Arabia," of which one critic said: "Lawrence emerged as the shining White Crusader, a character without blemish, a hero pure, brave, and humble . . . His name now became known, everywhere."

This was no ordinary motion picture, but an epic show that Lowell Thomas put on in New York, first at the Century Theatre and then at Madison Square Garden. For an important first he synchronized music and narration in a way never done before, using his own fabulous voice to tell the story. Of the hundreds of thousands who made up his audiences, there was an English impresario by the name of Percy Burton who dropped in one night, then met the narrator at lunch the following day. Impresario Percy Burton had a proposal. Since American audiences were so interested in two British heroes, he surmised that his own countrymen would be even more interested. Would Lowell Thomas come to London with his show?

Although he didn't take the offer seriously, the young American said yes, he'd like to come to London, provided that he could put on his show at Covent Garden Royal Opera House—and at the invitation of King George! The impresario, although startled at this, said he would see what he could do.

When the two parted, Lowell Thomas forgot about the matter. To his astonishment, just one month later, he received a cable complying with his demands.

After all, his show featured the story of two great Englishmen. As he said, up to that time only a little was known in London about the Palestine campaign, the capture of Jerusalem and Damascus. The British did know about Allenby, their brilliant cavalry general, but as for Lawrence, they didn't know he was on earth.

The London run turned out to be a sensation. He hired the Royal Welch Guards Band to play before and during the show. He also used one of Sir Thomas Beecham's opera scenes, the Moonlight on the Nile setting from "Joseph and His Brethren," and created the first stage prologue ever used with a film. One other novelty delighted his audiences, hearing the story of their own heroes told by an American with an American accent. It was novel, it was spectacular, it was exciting, it was amusing, it was wonderful!

The planned two weeks' engagement was prolonged for months and months. When the opera season could be held off no longer, Lowell Thomas moved his production into the huge Albert Hall—and filled it both afternoon and night. Who came to hear him? Everybody! King George came and Queen Mary, and the Prince of Wales led the applause. The prime minister appeared with his cabinet and all of the M. P.'s. Lord and Lady Allenby attended, Emir Feisal and his staff arrived, Premier Clemenceau and party from Paris. Such colorful people as Madame Melba and Tetrazzini, Israel Zangwill, George Bernard Shaw, Rudyard Kipling, Sir Johnston Forbes-Robertson, Ambassador John W. Davis and an endless stream of celebrities came backstage to meet the American troubadour. More than a million people in London alone came to look and listen. Even T. E. Lawrence came several times to hear his own story.

The mere physical strain of talking to great crowds twice a day over a four-month period told on Lowell Thomas, strong as he was. A doctor advised him to move into the country, so he and his wife took a place near Richmond. From his "digs" near Westminster Abbey, Lawrence would walk the twelve miles to see his friend. Frances Thomas studied shorthand and typing to help prepare the manuscript that was in process. Lawrence fitted in with their own modest appraisal of what they were accomplishing. Although Lawrence basked in the sunshine of all this popularity, he steadfastly refused the titles and decorations that were offered him. Yet he may have enjoyed being offered honors. Lowell Thomas quoted an old Turkish saying about Lawrence—"He had a genius for backing into the limelight."

Without his young American friend perhaps Lawrence would never have become a legend throughout the English-speaking world. Was he grateful? Once he wrote: "I saw your show last night. And, thank God, the lights were out."

Lawrence became the most talked about and painted personality in Great Britain. At Hammersley Hill, in his studio, Lowell Thomas has some striking portraits of the man he made so famous.

If Lawrence enjoyed fame he also was afraid of it. He accused Lowell Thomas of making him a hero "who had virtually destroyed the Ottoman empire single-handed." But the latter was not alone in his estimate of the man. Near East expert Gertrude Bell said of him, "He lit so many fires in cold rooms."

Later, Lawrence, on his return from Arabia, joined the R.A.F. under the assumed names of Ross and Shaw. He would go on, as long as life lasted, wise in his understanding, generous in his capacity to inspire people, and outgoing with his personal gifts. In his story there is triumph and tragedy, and, in the end, failure to free the Arabs. Although the Arab uprising did rout the Turks, it was years before Arabia became Arabia for the Arabs. For Lowell Thomas, Lawrence would always be the White Knight, the modern Crusader.

From London, a tour of the provinces followed: England, Scotland, Wales, and then on around the world. He was invited into the palaces of the maharajahs. He took time out to explore the wilds of Malaya, upper Burma and remote parts of India. As an exciting climax came an invitation from the Amir at Kabul to visit Afghanistan, at that time a forbidden land. He made journeys to Waziristan, to the Khyber Pass country, and beyond to the land of the Afghans, a memorable journey through the Khyber to King Amanullah in his palace in Kabul.

Following his account of "Lawrence in Arabia" came demands from publishers for other adventure tales which he managed to make time for. He has an adventure library of some fifteen thousand volumes, to which he has generously made his own contributions. Here they are, a whole shelf of books:

1. With Lawrence in Arabia
2. India—Land of the Black Pagoda
3. Beyond Khyber Pass
4. The First World Flight
5. Count Luckner, the Sea Devil
6. The Sea Devil's Fo'c's'le
7. European Skyways
8. Raiders of the Deep
9. Woodfill of the Regulars
10. The Hero of Vincennes
11. The Wreck of the Dumaru
12. Lauterbach of the China Sea
13. Rolling Stone
14. Tall Stories
15. Fan Mail
16. Kabluk of the Eskimo
17. This Side of Hell
18. The Boy's Life of Colonel Lawrence
19. Adventures in Afghanistan for Boys
20. Spain, the American Traveler's Handbook (in collaboration with Frank Schoonmaker)
21. Old Gimlet Eye: The Adventures of General Smedley Butler
22. The Untold Story of Exploration
23. Born to Raise Hell
24. Men of Danger

25. Kipling Stories and a Life of Kipling
26. Adventures Among Immortals
27. Seeing Canada With Lowell Thomas
28. Seeing India
29. Seeing Japan
30. Seeing Mexico
31. Hungry Waters
32. Wings Over Asia
33. Magic Dials
34. In New Brunswick You'll Find It
35. Soft Ball
36. How to Keep Mentally Fit
37. Stand Fast for Freedom
38. Pageant of Adventure
39. Pageant of Life
40. Pageant of Romance
41. These Men Shall Never Die
42. Back to Mandalay
43. Great True Adventures
44. Seven Wonders of the World
45. History as You Heard It
46. The Vital Spark
47. Sir Hubert Wilkins, a Biography
48. More Great True Adventures
49. Book of the High Mountains

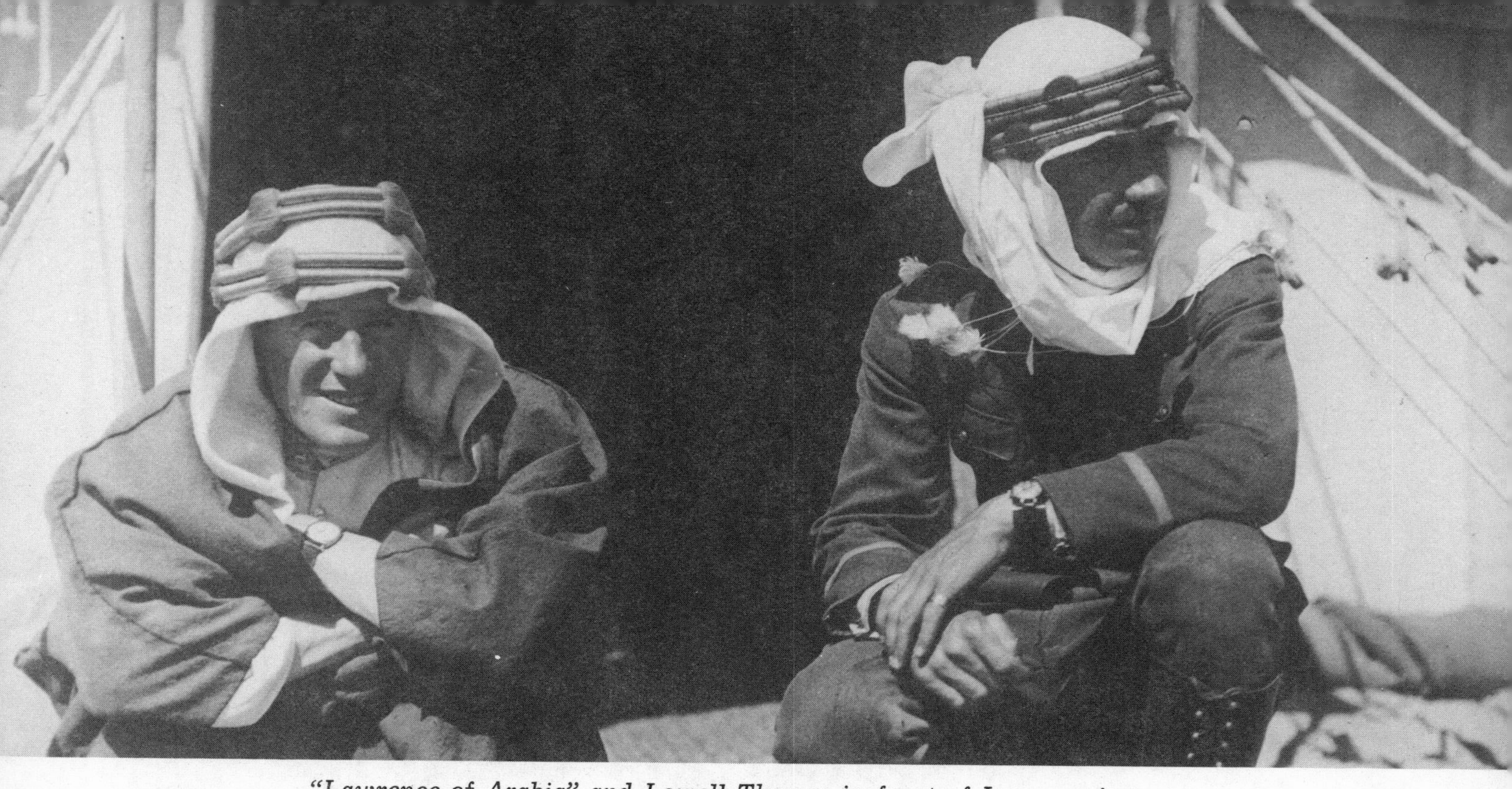

"Lawrence of Arabia" and Lowell Thomas in front of Lawrence's tent.

Lowell Thomas on Nero, 1938 or '39.

Lowell Thomas (left center) and the Prince of Wales, Edward VIII (right center).

Broadcasting from his first rural radio studio over 30 years ago.

Chapter Five

The Long Career Begins

The year 1930 stood out for young Lowell Thomas as one of the most significant years of his life because it marked the beginning of what was to be a long, exciting career before microphones and cameras.

The general public, familiar with his news program and TV series of the 1960's may find it incredible to realize that in 1930 there was only one daily radio broadcast in all the world. The broadcaster, however, was unforgettable, his staccato accent, his swift words pouring forth in a faster tempo than had previously been heard over the air—and his famous eye patch, the badge of a wound he received while a correspondent during World War I. This was Floyd Gibbons! Every evening he reeled off the news for his sponsor, "The Literary Digest." Then, after seven months, Floyd Gibbons and "The Literary Digest" were about to sever their relationship and the problem of who would succeed the colorful war correspondent was a poser. The sponsors had made what they considered an endless attempt to find the right man, but all the auditions spelled disappointment. They were about to give up radio advertising altogether when something happened. A CBS official had an inspiration. He knew just the man! He had heard him speak at Covent Garden Royal Opera House in London. This chap had been a war correspondent like Floyd Gibbons in World War I. He had also been a fantastically successful speaker who had brought fame to himself as well as to his two heroes, Allenby in Palestine, and Lawrence of Arabia. He had been the only observer to bring back an account of Allenby's capture of Jerusalem, the war in the desert, and his book, "With Lawrence in Arabia," was a world-wide best seller.

Who was this prospect? He was invited to come to New York for a tryout over CBS.

He did not realize it, but Lowell Thomas was about to sign up for the longest continuous run of any sponsored daily program of the electronic era. William S. Paley was the man behind the new choice that was to mean so much to "The Literary Digest," and the general public, as well as to such sponsors as The Sun Oil Company, for sixteen years, Standard Oil of California, Proctor & Gamble, as well as four divisions of General Motors over an unbroken period of thirty-five years in all. In two weeks the Floyd Gibbons contract would have reached an end. Time was of the essence.

Here is Lowell Thomas' own account of what transpired.

"Bill Paley saw what appeared to be an opportunity to land this major contract. He said to me, 'We must not fail. Your audition must be a masterpiece. To help you prepare a news broadcast, Columbia will loan you some of its best brains!' That gave me a jolt. I had been in public speaking all my life, and had been a newsman at home and abroad for twenty years. How could Columbia's 'best brains' help me prepare a fifteen-minute talk on the news of the day? But, I replied 'Okay. If you are going to loan me your finest brains, why I'll round up a few double domes from among my friends and we'll make it a real event.'

"Three days later I rented the penthouse atop the old Princeton Club in New York for an all-day session. Mr. Paley sent three of his stars and I brought mine. That is, I had called up my publisher at Garden City, Long Island, and said, 'Mr. Doubleday, have you any brains out there?' When I explained, he told me he would send in several of their 'brightest young men.' There were eight of us at that session at the Princeton Club, to discuss how to prepare a radio news broadcast, what to include, what to omit, and how to handle the news, so it would not be too much like what Floyd Gibbons had been doing. Our group was made up of the following geniuses and near-geniuses from CBS: Jesse Butcher, director of public relations (which, months later became the first radio news department). Butcher was a veteran newsman from the 'New York Times.' Then there was Nick Dawson who, they said, could do 'almost anything.' He had been an actor, a circus man, and had many talents. For a third, Mr. Paley sent Paul Kesten, a young executive who later became one of the heads of CBS. From Garden City Mr. Doubleday had sent in George Elliman and a young manuscript reader who, in those days, spent his spare time writing the verses for which he later became famous. His name, Ogden Nash.

"I also brought along Prosper Buranelli of crossword puzzle fame, who had been a star feature writer on the 'New York World.' And I included an old friend who had managed several road companies of my Allenby-Lawrence show and who, like Prosper and Ogden Nash, was later to become famous. His name—Dale Carnegie.

"This was in the prohibition era, and knowing something about the habits of newspapermen, I brought a flagon of something that might refresh them from our farm in Dutchess County, a region famous for its apples.

"Nick Dawson and Dale Carnegie immediately got into an argument as to how you should start a news broadcast. By midafternoon they still hadn't come to an agreement. I wonder if there ever was a gayer, more unsuccessful, more unproductive session than the one we had around that penthouse table. We never did get down to the business of writing script, except for a few paragraphs turned out by Ogden Nash.

"Late in the afternoon, seeing that we were fast arriving nowhere, I took the young woman stenographer I had hired to put down all the brilliant thoughts, and quietly disappeared, the others not even missing us. Hurriedly putting together some notes, I went before the CBS 'mike' at six o'clock and that was it. We landed the contract."

A week later, he succeeded Floyd Gibbons. And that date, September 29, 1930, marked the beginning of the long run, the longest continuous run of any daily sponsored network program in history. CBS radio president, Arthur Hull Hayes, a few years ago introduced him to an important audience in the electronic world as "Mr. Radio." Others have called him "Mr. Marco Polo"; and more recently, "Mister Cinerama." Even when out of the country, flying over the battle for Berlin, from Chungking in World War II, from Tibet, or the South Pole, he has managed to get his broadcast through. Millions of words, accurate and unprejudiced. At the end of each broadcast he adds a humorous or entertaining item to give his audience the feeling that it's still a pretty good world, even if the day's news has been grim and full of violence and tragedy, as it usually is.

The broadcasts began at a time of national depression. They continued through the Second World War and on through crisis after crisis—Korea, the Congo, Cuba, and a hundred more. To reread his broadcasts—more than a hundred bound volumes of them cover one wall of his handsome New York office—would be reading history. Lowell Thomas calls himself an optimist, but he is also a realist.

He has the gift for making important events stand out. To recite a few will give some idea of the momentous problems he has handled. In 1930 Hitler apes Mussolini and threatens to conquer Russia. Stalin collectivizes the lands of the Soviet Union. Talk of revolution against the monarchy in Spain, and in India Mahatma Gandhi advocates nonviolence. In 1932, Japanese military action in Manchuria spurs China to appeal to the League of Nations. In Spain, Alfonso XIII abdicates the throne, and in Germany, Hitler's Nazis disrupt the Reichstag. Stalin massacres many Kulaks, the rich peasants. At home, President Hoover declares a moratorium on Germany's World War I war debts.

Along with his fantastic clarity of expression, he has the rare ability to tell a story, and with this goes that marvelous gift of diction. From the start he was welcomed in homes in all parts of the country, and among all classes. He made no attempt to imitate the Floyd Gibbons machine gun staccato style.

Lowell Thomas, encouraged by his friend and co-worker Prosper Buranelli, preferred to be his natural self. His greeting, "Good evening everybody," always sounded as though it came from a friendly neighbor. It was like having somebody burst into one's house with exciting news he could hardly wait to tell. The greeting was a natural.

How about an ending for each broadcast? Floyd Gibbons would be apt to say, "Now let's catch a ship for China—here we go, boys and girls."

Prosper Buranelli, sitting broad and smiling in Lowell Thomas' quarters, shook his head at all the fanciful, imaginative suggestions. He said, "Only you will know what would be right for you, L. T."

" 'So long until tomorrow' suits me," said Lowell, and that was that. It seemed to be something brand new on the air at that time, in those days of long ago, and it caught on. Nothing could have been more effective.

Coming just before Amos and Andy undoubtedly helped him get off to a flying start with countless millions of listeners. But his own style, the swift march of world events and the novelty of it all combined to cause his audience to grow and grow until literally everyone in America knew his voice. In 1932 he announced the election of Franklin D. Roosevelt as President of the United States, and told the tragic story of the Lindbergh baby kidnaping. He followed the trend in foreign conspiracies and at home the coming of "The New Deal." The closing of the banks to prevent financial panic was alarming news, as was the disruptions abroad with Hitler gaining power. Drought ravaged much of our southwest. By 1935 Mussolini was invading Ethiopia. And then, calamity struck the world, with Hitler's march into the Rhineland. To offset the news of wars and rumors of war, Lowell Thomas had one of the great love stories of all time—Edward VIII abdicating the British throne to marry Wallis Simpson, the two going into exile as the Duke and Duchess of Windsor, and the coronation of another King George, which Lowell "covered" so dramatically from London.

At home, the 1936 election brought another political victory for Lowell Thomas' Hyde Park, Dutchess County neighbor. Wars continue—Civil War in Spain, Japan seizes Shanghai and bombs the American gunboat Panay. Stalin continues persecutions in Russia. At home there is much controversy over the possible packing of the Supreme Court. Lowell Thomas, following his original Literary Digest formula which seemed to "come naturally" to him, simply stated facts and let them speak for themselves. There was stark tragedy in the news—the burning of the German dirigible Hindenberg at Lakehurst, New Jersey . . . John D. Rockefeller, billionaire founder of Standard Oil and world's foremost philanthropist, dies. By 1940 Hitler had turned what many had thought a "phony war" into the grimmest war men have even known. At Dunkirk, most of the British army on the continent is saved, and Winston Churchill coins an immortal phrase in praise of the men who fought and died there. Mussolini joins Hitler, attacks Greece, and is defeated. The Finnish war ends but Stalin's terms are harsh. Trotsky is brutally assassinated in Mexico.

At home, President Roosevelt runs for still a third term, this time against Wendell Willkie, as he promises that our troops will not go to war. At last he puts an embargo on those all-important scrap iron shipments to Japan.

Then, as their emissaries were treacherously talking peace in Washington, the Japanese air force was making its surprise attack at the American naval and air base in Hawaii. Wake, Guam, and Hong Kong fall, and battles raged in the Philippines and Malaya. Singapore goes too. General MacArthur fights valiantly with a pitifully inadequate force.

Meanwhile, Hitler has turned on his erstwhile Russian partner. The weird Rudolph Hess case gets the headlines, the story of the man who flew to Scotland with a proposal for a common front against Russia. He becomes a prisoner of the British . . . President Roosevelt signs the Lend-Lease Bill, and the Neutrality Act is repealed. At sea, the President confers with Winston Churchill.

Each night in 1942, Lowell Thomas took his audience around the world, the world he knew so intimately. Much of the news was so shocking it stunned us —the loss of Singapore for the British and the fall of the Philippines for the Americans. Who will ever forget the heroic defense of Bataan and Corregidor, and the Bataan death march that so aroused the nation?

Then all hearts were lifted as Lowell Thomas told the dramatic story of the bombing of Tokyo by Jimmy Doolittle and his Mitchell bomber crews. The Navy wins the battles of the Coral Sea and Midway Island. The Marines return to Guadalcanal, after many a hideous jungle battle. In Russia, the Germans are stopped cold at Stalingrad. Marshal Rommel, the "Desert Fox," is caught in North Africa between the British army under Montgomery and the Americans under Eisenhower.

Audiences now were hearing with relief how Hitler lost the French fleet when it was deliberately scuttled by its own crews.

By 1943 Lowell Thomas at long last could report the tide had turned against the Rome-Berlin Axis. He also reported that major political meeting, the Teheran Conference, the first get-together of Roosevelt, Churchill and Stalin. General Eisenhower proclaims D-Day, and there is a second front in Europe.

By 1944 Hitler's power begins to crumble; he commits suicide; Mussolini is captured and brutally executed; Germany surrenders unconditionally, and a few months later the atom bomb ends Japan's mad dream of world empire. All of these Lowell described from the scene—from Italy, Germany, France, and the Far East.

Meanwhile, President Roosevelt dies and is succeeded by Vice President Truman. Lowell Thomas points out two great problems that the country faces: the matter of the atomic bomb which, although it forced the surrender of Japan, now hangs as a terrifying sword of Damocles over the human race. Then comes the unfortunate Yalta Conference of Roosevelt, Churchill, and Stalin, following which Stalin goes on breaking solemn promises.

With the war over in 1946, America faces vast new problems posed by the Russian Communists. In 1947 Lowell Thomas explains how Stalin does not want a proper international settlement.

The Marshall Plan goes into effect. In 1948 Harry S. Truman is formally elected President. A Korean incident leads to war. The most dramatic event of 1951, Truman's dismissal of MacArthur, one of the great military figures of all time, and the latter's eloquent farewell speech before Congress.

In 1952 President Truman is succeeded by President Eisenhower. Stalin dies, and in 1955 a new name in Communist headlines—the name of Nikita Khrushchev, erstwhile lieutenant of the brutal Stalin.

But now along with more news of horror and man's continuing savagery, in 1953 Lowell Thomas has the relief of narrating the beautiful story of the crowning of young Queen Elizabeth with all the pomp and ceremony of age-old tradition in Westminster Abbey.

The melodramatic McCarthy hearings, with the censure of the stormy Wisconsinite by the Senate and the Senator's attack on President Eisenhower for expressing approval of that censorship! Minor and major events are given much space. Ford's guaranteed wage for its employees starting a trend, the effectiveness of the Salk polio vaccine, and the President's announcement that he intends to conquer outer space through our scientists. . . . Albert Einstein, wizard mathematical physicist, one of the real giants of our era, dies.

The political campaign in which Richard Nixon, Republican candidate, loses the presidential election by a narrow margin that places John F. Kennedy and his glamorous Jacqueline in the White House. The Cuban situation continues difficult as refugees pour into the United States.

All during those three decades of five-day-a-week broadcasting, Lowell Thomas has rarely, if ever, been away from his work. Even when out of the country he has managed to send in material from everywhere—from Tibet, from the South Pole, the North Pole, from among the Stone Age people of inner wild New Guinea, from the Congo, the Amazon jungle, from Central Asia, he tells the story of this modern era and of his own fabulous adventures. The response from his vast audiences brings its daily avalanche of mail, some critical, some in praise.

Here is a message that must have warmed his heart, from one Friedrich Newman, a Christian Jew who wrote a book about his miraculous escape from death in a Hitler gas chamber:

"A foreigner in a dark, cold room. It was 6:45 p.m. I felt wretchedly lonely and yearned for a kind human voice to warm my frozen heart. I wanted to contact humanity mechanically and for the first time turned on an American radio.

"I heard a voice so cheerful, musical, warm and human as never before in any country and any language. This voice spoke about the war in Europe, without hatred against those who started that war. This voice combined with its unusual speed a perfect clarity and gentle humor. Every word sounded like a bell and was easy to understand. This voice was confident of our final victory. It was the fascinating voice of Lowell Thomas."

On the humorous side there are always the listeners who are sticklers for pronunciation. His unaffected, perhaps slightly Western accent comes in for occasional barbs.

Here is a sample correction, as he calls it, from Ontario. This was when the Pews of Sun Oil were his sponsors and Hugh James his announcer:

"I suppose it is too late to save the 'u' sound from practical extinction in American English. It isn't NOO, it's NEW. It isn't DOO, it's DEW. Try this one on your microphone: HUGH HEWED A FEW NEW PEWS IN THE DEW."

An Illinois woman adds her bit:

"I walked down the AVENOO and bought a NOOSEPAPER at the NOOSESTAND and read about the CONSTITOOTION. It was TOOSDAY and on my route of DOOTY, I bought a TOOLIP on that DOOEY morning. I also bought a radio TOOB and TOONED in some nice TOONS."

Thus Lowell Thomas is responsible, not only for the words he speaks, but the way in which he speaks them. Most Americans like him for the way he is, but he frankly admits he has learned much from his critical listeners—and he adds, "from my wife who has an ear for everything that isn't quite perfect!"

On an occasion of a sponsor's inviting free telegrams for a certain broadcast as comment, there was amazing response. Even Lowell Thomas, the optimist, was overwhelmed at the number he received . . . over 262,000! The greatest single response, ever, before or since.

Having long been a celebrity, perhaps it was inevitable that Lowell Thomas would one day be snared into the sentimental tear-jerker program, Ralph Edwards' TV show "This Is Your Life."

How did it happen? Oh, they trapped him at a banquet. Floodlights, suddenly Ralph Edwards rushes forward, microphone in hand, shouting, "Lowell Thomas, this is your life!"

But Lowell is not amused. He growls, "It looks to me like a sinister conspiracy."

Ralph Edwards' "star" obviously was not going to be too cooperative. When he hears the voice of his sister, Pherbia Thomas Thornburg, onstage saying, "Father insisted that you learn every rock and mineral in that mining camp," he replies, "Maybe, but I also knew every saloon in Cripple Creek."

Edwards might have explained that young Lowell as a boy had delivered and sold newspapers in the rowdy mining camp; instead, he rushed Mrs. Thomas on stage and told a sentimental story of their courtship.

Sitting next to her husband, Fran whispers in his ear and Lowell, turning to the audience, says, "Want to know what she whispered to me? She wanted to know, '**Must** I kiss you, here?' "

From that moment for Ralph Edwards everything fell apart. Roly poly Prosper Buranelli grinned at his sour-faced boss and asked, "How mad are you?"

"Prosper," the boss said, "you've had too much to drink."

"Too much?" replied Prosper, "Not enough! Let me outta here!"

By this time, as one critic reported, everything was out of focus but the camera. It was a near riot from then on, with viewers enjoying it as never before. The whole country roared with laughter. L. T. had taken over. As for Ralph Edwards, his show was so wrecked that he couldn't even get in the usual commercials.

The next night Lowell Thomas explained, sheepishly rather than apologetically, on his own evening radio program: "If I seemed a bit sardonic, it was because it was so unexpected, and I just didn't like the whole idea. No tear-jerker for me."

"That poor man!" exclaimed some in the TV audience, and they didn't mean Lowell Thomas. Actually, in the end Ralph Edwards needed no commiseration, especially after he saw the program's rating for that evening — an all-time high, and later the two have become warm friends. Until that night they had never met.

Chapter Six

So Long Until Tomorrow

This borrowed farewell after a day in snowy mountains may well express the exuberant good-bye-for-now of the sports fan.

To golfers Lowell Thomas is widely known as a golfer who has carried his enthusiasm so far that he has built two courses, one of which has become famous because it includes five overwater holes and the longest hole in the world, an 800-yard, par 7. True, he does like the so-called "Royal and Ancient" game, and is a member of such unusual clubs as The Royal and Ancient at St. Andrews, Scotland; The Low Tide Golf Club on Wake Island in the far Pacific; the Farthest North Club in Alaska; the challenging Pine Valley Club in the sand and scrub pine of southern New Jersey; as well as local golf clubs near where he lives. But actually, his first choice is skiing, and his favorite setting is any high, snowy mountain in the Andes, the Alps, New Zealand, the Himalayas, the Green Mountains, the White Mountains, the Adirondacks, the Laurentians, the Tetons, or the High Sierra. But if he had any preference it probably would be for somewhere in the Colorado or Utah Rockies, or in Alaska, where he often goes.

Some say he has done more to popularize skiing than any other sportsman in America. It is the exercise he most enjoys, and for him it is not seasonal. It ceases to be a winter sport, for he will hunt for high mountains or go to the Southern Hemisphere to find snow in the summer. Some five million Americans are skiing today, he reminds the public, with men, women and children enjoying the sport equally. Skiing, once thought of as a violent sport for top athletes, has progressed to where an ex-Panama Canal engineer, Smith-Johannsen, over eighty, will outski many of the younger generation.

Ski lovers will tell the world that anyone bitten by the ski bug may find that he is a "natural" for this spectacular sport. It was back in 1916 that Lowell Thomas caught the fever. Since then America's most famous commentator and newscaster has had a way of telling about the delights of skiing that makes it seem a way of life—a dynamic, thrilling, soul-satisfying way of life.

It was during World War I that Lowell Thomas first strapped on a pair of skis. He was, at that time, attached to a high-mountain brigade of the Italian Alpini, who were holding a line separating northern Italy from Austria in the Alps, at 13,000 feet on Monte Rosa. That was his first exposure to it.

That there were experts across the valley who one day would be his ski friends did not occur to him. He had no idea that serving with the Austrians over there was a skier destined to become world famous—Hannes Schneider. The officer in charge of the refugio where Lowell Thomas had been dropped by a basket cableway, was a sportsman who a few years later was to make his name in Canada. He was a colorful figure, a nobleman to begin with, part Russian, part English, and of the Italian nobility. Tall, straight, and handsome, he was known to skiers as "the Markee" and he actually was the Marquis degli d'Albizzi. In World War II he was helping his young American friend with an area where airmen returning from combat went for rest and rehabilitation. Skiing seemed to do wonders for them, and the "Markee" was the maestro of the Lowell Thomas Quaker Hill ski slopes.

Lowell Thomas began skiing in earnest in January 1926, after a speaking tour of Canada. He began to ski at home, on the slopes of Quaker Hill, with a captain of the Swedish Army. Many snows had filled the valleys since that first attempt at skiing in the Alps as a young war correspondent. Fortune had smiled on him. His "With Lawrence in Arabia" had proved a sensation, a book that was to go into over a hundred editions. His German sea raider material, the story of Count Luckner, the Sea Devil, was an equally spectacular success, and he was in constant demand as a speaker.

While on tour in Canada, he had purchased three pairs of skis and ski poles. The reason for the purchase —because he and his wife were about to entertain their first royalty, Prince Wilhelm, second son of King Gustav of Sweden. Here was a visitor, he reasoned, who would surely be an expert on skis. After all, the Prince hailed from "the very cradle of the sport."

But it didn't quite turn out that way. The Prince not only didn't care for skiing, his main interest was in equatorial Africa, and he spent most of the ten days of his visit in the new home the Lowell Thomases had just acquired. Sub-zero weather was not for him. He preferred equatorial Africa.

However, the visit wasn't a complete disappointment from this standpoint. Lowell got in some skiing with Prince Wilhelm's aid, the Swedish army captain. Says the host, "Having skied from early boyhood, the Captain was an expert on cross-country and he gave me my first informal lesson."

Several years later Lowell Thomas had his first formal instruction. It was the winter of 1932 at Lake Placid, New York. Here the first Winter Olympic Games ever staged in this country were in progress.

At the Lake Placid Club there was one instructor, Erling Strom, a handsome Norwegian, one of the first, if not the first, ever to hold ski classes in North America. After Lowell watched the skiing of two Norwegian champions, Birger and Sigmund Ruud, he decided to sign up for lessons. These Scandinavian champions had inspired him.

A lasting friendship developed between Strom and pupil. During the succeeding thirty-two years they often skied together. Here at Lake Placid another friendship grew between Lowell and the late Olympic bobsled champion, Herbert Stevens, one of the creators of the Whiteface Mountain Ski Development in the Adirondacks, who also caught the ski virus, as did nearly everyone who came in contact with Lowell Thomas for the next twenty years.

When asked to name the pros who had been most inspiring and helpful, he did not hesitate. He is always enthusiastic and generous with praise.

In the early thirties there was what he called the "Austrian invasion" to New Hampshire, the Cannon Mountain area. They were imported by Katherine Peckett of Sugar Hill. With his son, Lowell went to learn the Arlberg technique. Here his instructors were mainly Kurt Thalhammer and Sig Buchmayr, at first, then Otto Lang, Benno Rybizka, and others in the Franconia and North Conway areas. They were followed by the late great Hannes Schneider, often called the father of modern skiing. His story is a dramatic one, for the great sportsman was a prisoner in a Nazi concentration camp. A well-known financier, Harvey Gibson, who had influence in international banking circles, finally secured his release. Welcome hands were outstretched to greet him when he arrived at North Conway, accompanied by champion Toni Matt, and his own son, Herbert Schneider.

The list of top ski figures with whom Lowell Thomas has skied is endless. Some few should be mentioned, for the great new American sport is forever indebted to their genius.

Both before and after the Mansfield chair lift was built at Stowe, he skied with Jacques Charmoz, Sepp Ruschp, Lionel Hayes, Kerr Sparks and Otto Hollaus.

Other names stand out: Friedl Pfeifer, Hans Hauser, Luggi Foegger, Sigi Engl, Otto Steiner, Wiggi Hasher, Dick Durrance, the Engens, Alf, Sverre and Corey, Fred Iselin, Stein Eriksen, Ernie McCullough, Kay Smith and Zayne Doyle, Toni Matt and Jim McConkey, Steve Bradley, Bill Klein, Gretchen and Don Fraser. and others in the West. In the East he accompanied several European stars in their first ski jaunts in this country: Emile Allais, Sepp Froelich, Raidar Anderson, Tom Murstad, Heinrich Harrer, Pepi and Franz Gabl, Hans Faulkner, Peter Gabriel, Johnny Litchfield, Michael Fuersinger, Fritz Wiessner and Sel Hannah, Neil Robinson and Sally Pabst. There were six who proved constant companions: Jack and Gladys Sawyer, Chris and Mary Young, Jim Parker, and "Iron Man" Bob Kehoe.

When asked to name his favorite of all the great skiers he has known, Lowell Thomas refuses. He would not put one above the other. He says, "Each is an expert in his own way. Each has his own personality, his own way of imparting knowledge of the sport."

When the matter of equipment came up in an interview, Lowell was less evasive, but, as one fellow sportsman said, his taste maybe seemed too all-inclusive.

He said, "I suspect I'd be better off with only one pair of skis instead of two dozen. Most of mine are standard makes. But some are experimental, including a pair of 'goonies.' Did you ever see Prince Bernhard go whirling by on his? Or Jimmy Madden of Boston who is the original 'goony' wizard? . . . It may be funny, but it's also spectacular."

How about the person who can have only one pair or, at the most, two pairs of skis? And what of bindings, safety or otherwise? Lowell Thomas advised skiers to purchase any type of ski that suits them. As for the so-called "safety" bindings, he confessed that sometimes he used them, sometimes not. And he had had broken bones both with and without.

From the Lake Placid and Sugar Hill days he now looks back with pleasure on those first exciting days in the snow belt and that first rope tow at Woodstock. He recalls Fred Pabst and his pioneering, and Kate Peckett with her imported yodelers from the Tyrol. Soon American skiing radically changed from jumping and ski touring.

Professional and venturesome amateurs now were learning to ski like the natives in the Austrian, Swiss and French Alps. That meant swift running down mountains and high-speed turns.

He would have liked to bring skiing to Radio City or to Madison Avenue, but, lacking that possibility, he took his broadcasting to the mountains, the Adirondacks, the Green Mountains, the White Mountains, the Laurentians, the Rockies, the Sierras, and so on.

He did this five evenings a week, and soon he was being picked up by remote control from the Lake Placid Club, from Smuggler's Notch at the foot of Mt. Mansfield in Vermont, from Mont Tremblant Lodge in Quebec, where there is a "Lowell Thomas Run" on the highest peak in the Laurentians, from Sun Valley, from the ancient opera house at Aspen, from the railway station at Donner Pass in the High Sierra, from the Tenth Mountain Division area in the Rockies at Camp Hale, from the molybdenum mine at Climax, Colorado, Mount Hood in Oregon, and Alaska! Guest skiers more often than not sat in on these broadcasts, causing considerable upset among the engineers as ski boots tangled with wire cable. Outside, snow might be falling or even a blizzard raging, but the familiar ringing voice of Lowell Thomas gave out the news of the world.

The result of all this broadcasting from ski resorts had pleasant results. First of all, it enabled him to get in a good deal of skiing—his primary aim but not necessarily a selfish aim, for the broadcasts scintillated with good humor and dry wit. Secondly, the resort places were getting some mighty fine free advertising along with the manufacturers who sold ski equipment. Lastly and most important, among the millions who listened in, there came to be many converts to a wholesome and healthful sport.

For all this he had to be accompanied by something of an entourage. While his working cast was held to a minimum, there had to be a network engineer, a traveling secretary who could double at broadcast time, and a telegraph operator.

Most of the time the broadcasts went through without incident. But there were some uncertain moments. In a town near Lake Placid one evening a fire blazed through the business district, knocking out the key trunk telephone lines. Up until 6:40 he was not sure but what he would be talking to himself and not to his usual audience of millions. But thanks to the telephone company, the broadcast did get through. Their men worked a miracle with a last-minute hookup from Lake Placid to somewhere in New England—and finally to New York, and on out over the network.

A different sort of hazard occurred in the Laurentians on beautiful Mont Tremblant where, after a long day in the sharp winter air, at forty below, his voice suddenly vanished.

Let Lowell himself describe his predicament: "There I was, trying to do my usual, when all of a sudden—silence! My lips continued to form the words, but no sound."

By great good fortune Lowell, Jr., an expert skier and an experienced speaker, was there—not only there, but seated at the table timing the broadcast. His father shoved the microphone and script in front of the young man. Whereupon L. T., Jr. continued where his father left off. The broadcast finished on the nose, with few who were listening able to tell the difference.

Mont Tremblant, as far north as skiers go in the Laurentians, is the Joe and Mary Ryan story, but L. T. is an important part of it too.

One amusing incident stands out like a prologue for the Ryans. To broadcast from the land of the Habitant during the years when the area was being developed, the Canadian Pacific Railway station at St. Jovite seemed the only place. The main waiting room was not available. There was a small room reserved for MESDAMES. Would it do? It would. The truckload of radio equipment was crowded into the Ladies'

Room, and from that room deep in the province of Quebec the broadcast went out to all North America.

About Mont Tremblant: that in itself is a story and belongs back in the mid-thirties. From the windows of the Wheeler's Gray Rocks Inn, a friendly chalet, Lowell Thomas could see the mountain named Tremblant. He wanted to see it closer, and made his wishes vocal to Tom Wheeler, who offered to fly him over and land him on the frozen lake at the base of the mountain. From there they could reach the summit with climbing skins on their skis; Harry Wheeler going along as a guide.

A husky young man, overhearing their plans, asked to join them. L. T. said he could come. There was just enough room in the plane. The young man's name, Joe Ryan, of Philadelphia.

The flight was a success, also the climb. "What a view!" exclaimed Joe Ryan, and then added, "But there's one thing wrong with this mountain. It's too darn hard to climb it. But I think I'll fix that."

He did, and the fixing made ski history.

So that was why one of the major ski trails was named "Lowell Thomas Run."

Nor was this the first and only trail named for him in the ski world. Later there was one on Whiteface Mountain in the Adirondacks, also a ski jump on Tenderfoot Hill, near Cripple Creek, Colorado, where he spent his boyhood. Oh yes, and Polar Explorer MacMillan named an island in the Arctic for him—Lowell Thomas Island. Even more spectacular are the Lowell

Thomas Mountains down near the South Pole, placed on the map by Captain Finn Ronne, Antarctic explorer.

Outside of Alaska and the Yukon the Mont Tremblant Ski Club was the one farthest north. So why not found a ski club farthest south? In 1943 when Lowell, Jr., a lieutenant in the air force, was stationed near Tucson, Arizona, his father visited him. As he looked down at the Santa Catalina Mountains some nine thousand feet above sea level, he thought surely there must be skiing in those mountains. The natives said no, but the Thomases proved them wrong—much to the distress of the local chamber of commerce, which called itself the Tucson Sunshine Club.

"Some of the officials blew their tops. Couldn't quite see the idea of promoting winter sports in an area where people came to escape the ice and snow and anything associated with it."

However, a ski club was organized called "The Suaharo," the name of the giant cactus that grows in the region, with a most impressive list of officials and honorary members, such as American champions Dick Durrance, Art Devlin, Hal Burton, skier and writer, Hannes Schneider, Otto Lang, Alf Engen, Erling Strom, Bill Eldred, the publisher of "Ski," and Darryl Zanuck, and a hundred other stars of that day.

After the world war, with Europe out of the sports running, the style became "Ski in America first." These places became familiar in summer: from Mad River to Yosemite and remote Mineral King, Manchester to Snoqualime, Alta, the Sugar Bowl, Squaw Valley, and

Colorado's San Juan. Some skied in Chile, the Columbia ice fields, and on the Juneau, Alaska icecap.

Because he enjoyed the sport so much himself, Lowell Thomas was given to proselyting, winning converts among movie stars, military men, and diplomats. Naturally he longed to have his neighbors share his enthusiasm, especially one neighbor, Thomas E. Dewey, then governor of the state of New York. But he seemed to get nowhere.

Then one morning in mid-January Mr. Dewey called, saying briskly, "Well, I am now ready for that ski lesson you've been promising me. Let's go!"

Lowell Thomas was dubious. "The Governor couldn't have picked a worse day," he remembered. "It was mid-January, and we'd had the usual thaw followed by the usual freeze-up. Our local ski slope, on Strawberry Hill, was a sheet of ice . . . no place for a beginner!"

At that time genial Jim Parker was ski instructor at Strawberry Hill. He did his best. The Governor did his best. But as Lowell Thomas later reported, "The Governor got a dim view of skiing, viewing it from a prone position most of the time.

The two presumably remained friends, but Lowell Thomas says, "Now when I am with Tom Dewey, I avoid talk about skiing."

Once he was challenged by a most unusual ski trip. The superintendent of the Camp Bird mine near the town of Ouray in Colorado sent him the invitation.

Here is his account of what happened:

"At the appointed hour we arrived at the mine entrance. Here, garbed in slickers and helmets, and carrying our skis, the superintendent, Lowell, Jr., and I climbed aboard the usual mine train and were carried to a point deep inside the mountain. Here we entered a cage and were whisked to a higher level. We left this for another train, then up again in a cage. Now as we neared the top we entered a long, low tunnel, almost impassible because of ice from surface water. Through this we crawled on our hands and knees, pushing our skis ahead of us. At last we emerged in brilliant sunshine into what is called the Chicago Basin at the top of the range. We were in a vast bowl at almost 14,000 feet, near the crest of the San Juan Mountains. On every side stretched an expanse of snow-covered slopes as impressive as anything I had ever seen. We snapped on our skis and started down. What followed was one of the longest runs I ever made, and one of the most nerve-racking because of the accompanying roar of spring avalanches."

A dangerous sport? Sometimes, of course! Every spring, for years, he and his die-hard friends made a pilgrimage to Tuckerman Ravine near the summit of Mount Washington, in New Hampshire. With other skiers he would climb to the foot of Headwall, then struggle on, slipping, often spilling head over heels.

The most dangerous part is when a skier makes his way to a dizzy shelf at the edge of the Mt. Washington Cone. Here you try to "run the Headwall," a thousand-foot sheer precipice that can only be skied by experts in April and May.

Lowell Thomas one early April day . . . his fiftieth birthday, attempted to run the Headwall. He had some notable skiers with him—Sepp Ruschp, Kerr Sparks, Lionel Hayes, Bob Bourdon, Otto Hollaus and Sigurd Winsness, who had escaped from Norway when the Nazis invaded his country. In fact, he had fled on skis via Lapland and Finland, to Bolshevik Russia, and on across Siberia.

Lowell Thomas has described his celebration of his fiftieth birthday on skis on Mount Washington, as follows:

"After a rest on the summit," he reminisces, "we sped down the smooth cone. Then over the Headwall—over that cliff, where as you try to look over and pick a route, it's so steep you can't even see what is just below you. For the first two hundred feet, no trouble! Then, a crevasse! I don't know quite what happened. But in a flash I was going end over end. A fall that continued for the remaining eight hundred feet! Once you lose your balance on the Tuckerman Headwall, there isn't a thing you can do about it. Anyhow, I had proved a point, whatever it was."

His companions were amused by their fellow skier as he spun, only slightly bruised, to a stop far down at the foot of the wall. He had proved his point, that a half-century mark cannot deter a determined skier.

It was after his serious injury while on the Tibetan trip that he suffered one ski casualty. He called it a minor one. It did not happen on Tuckerman Headwall, but on gentle Strawberry Hill at Pawling. He had broken a leg on the Tibetan trail; he broke the other leg at home. He was making a run on "unbreakable" crust when, near the bottom of the slope, a ski broke through—and a bone fractured . . . but no fracture ever interrupted his broadcasts.

Ever the optimist, he has faith, not only in himself, but in his fellow men. He is ever willing to help, in any way he can, especially to further interest in his favorite sport.

In the Hammersley Hill studio there are scores of fascinating mementos decorating the walls. Someone has left a precious fragment of stained glass near the owner's desk. It is the only religious note among all the gay, often humorous tributes to golfing, skiing, and broadcasting.

It is the scene from the New Testament in which Christ calms the waves for his frightened disciples.

The legend? WHY ARE YE FEARFUL, O YE OF LITTLE FAITH?

Anyone whose life has even remotely touched the life of Lowell Thomas realizes that he is first and foremost a man of great faith. He is a believer.

Chapter Seven

Cinerama and the Parthenon

Next came a revolution in the art of motion pictures. When "This Is Cinerama" opened at a Broadway theater in New York, it was the beginning of "The Wide Screen Era," the fourth major stage in film history. The exact date was September 30th, 1952, thirty-two years to the day from when he had started his radio career. The inventor of Cinerama was Fred Waller, a veteran film technician, but without the help of Lowell Thomas his invention might never have gotten off the ground. The help of Lowell Thomas and his associates insured production and ended worries of deferment that had been plaguing the inventor.

The key to it was peripheral vision, greater breadth and scope. But there was more than mere theater pleasure to the discoverer. There was a practical aspect as well. Fred Waller developed a gunnery trainer that probably saved countless American aviators' lives. The Air Force put up needed funds, and during the Second World War airmen sat at machine-gun mounts surrounded by a big circular screen. To get the effect he wanted, Waller had hooked up eleven projectors, all synchronized so that a gunner could see both enemy and friendly aircraft. In simulated practice they viewed, aimed, and fired their guns, becoming familiar with tactics they would encounter in war, both in the Atlantic and the Pacific. The Waller Gunnery Trainer proved invaluable.

Waller worked on his project for fourteen years, but never got it out of the laboratory. Even when stereophonic sound was added by Hazard Reeves, the movie moguls turned the invention down because a seven-channel, seven-sound track with its projectors and a wide curved screen could not fit into an ordinary movie house.

Here was where Lowell Thomas came in. "Buzz" Reeves, an old friend, invited him to look at it, and he was "sold" at once. As usual, his ideas were big.

"I am not tied down to motion picture orthodoxy," he explained. "Forget the small movie house. Put it in a Broadway theater, along the lines of a regular Broadway show." Merian Cooper, a Hollywood producer—and friend, played a vital part in this. Also Frank M. Smith, the financial wizard.

As nearly everybody knows, the Broadway opening of "This Is Cinerama" got off to a stunning success. The audience was not merely an onlooker, but a participant, thrilling to the dizzy curves of the roller coaster, riding in a gondola in Venice, in an airplane over and far down in the Grand Canyon of the Colorado—experiencing instead of merely seeing! The "New York Times" published its review on the front page—some-

Homer Croy, Lowell Thomas and Prosper Buranelli at Western Union headquarters, pursuing responses to a broadcast story.

Captain Rickenbacher, General Doolittle and Lowell Thomas

President Eisenhower and Lowell Thomas

Edward R. Murrow, former Governor Thomas E. Dewey, Gene Sarazen, Lowell Thomas and Sam Snead

thing that had never happened before in the world of movie reviews. The success of "Cinerama" was big enough to be page one news.

It was thrilling news to Fred Waller, too. The man of many hobbies had worked for many years as an expert for Paramount, doing things no one else could do. Now his life's work came to a climax. By using three projectors and a wide, curved screen, he had startled the world.

Three-dimensional, yes. The corporate structure that made up the business exploitation was also three-dimensional. One company owning the patents, another making equipment, and a third the production and display of films. When Lowell Thomas expanded to other cities, it cost $250,000 to revise and equip each theater.

"This Is Cinerama" ran on Broadway at theatrical prices for nearly two and a half years, breaking all records. It played in cities across the United States and abroad; London, Paris, Tokyo, at the Damascus Fair and the Bangkok Fair. Dollars rolled into the Cinerama treasury by the millions.

Lowell Thomas was as certain of the success of "The Seven Wonders of the Modern World" as though he had already seen the profits. When it was decided to film it, he again was both producer and narrator. To do this, he had to secure a leave of absence from General Motors. Charles Collingwood, Douglas Edwards and other talented younger men were to take his place on the nightly news program while he himself sent back tapes from whatever part of the world he chanced to be in.

Now he was off! In the airliner that was carrying him on his search for the modern Seven Wonders, he sat down with an oblong box and talked with a microphone into an electric tape recorder. These tapes could be shipped back by the plane on which he had traveled to Shannon, Ireland.

He had already planned to show the ancient wonders as prologue to the modern wonders in paintings. This to be done by Mario Larrinaga, who was not only a top-ranking artist but a scholar as well. The only one of the seven ancient wonders still standing, the Pyramids of Ghiza, could be filmed on the spot with he himself doing the narration live.

But it was possible to find human marvels close at hand, and he thought of his jet-flying friend Charley Blair, the trans-Atlantic pilot who shuttled back and forth between New York and Shannon, Ireland, on the Pan American clipper, Seven Seas. Charley Blair was the only man who had ever flown solo across the North Pole. It was in a P-51, a World War II fighter plane with special gas tanks. He made his unique flight from near Comso Fjord in Norway to Fairbanks, in the heart of Alaska, in order to demonstrate his own new theory on the way to use celestial navigation in remote regions where there was no radio aid. So Lowell Thomas told about him in his first broadcast as he set forth on his search for the Seven Wonders. "He's tall, handsome, gentle and gay. He looks like a youngster, and here's his record: more than 22,000 hours in the air, more than four million miles, plus piloting planes across the Atlantic more than six hundred times.

"I've always been interested in what unusual people do when they're not doing what they usually do. As the captain of this Pan Am airliner, Charley Blair is in the air approximately two weeks out of every month. Now what do you suppose he does the rest of the time—the other two weeks? I'll wager you'd never guess.

"He flies jets, the latest Sabre jets. He has over six hundred hours on them, and recently he checked out in the huge B-32, a six-engine superjet. He just likes to fly, and, above all, he likes to fly jets. Since his record solo flight across the North Pole, he has been a special consultant to the U. S. Government—and, as you would expect, a consultant to the Strategic Air Force.

"If my fellow passengers knew the record of their skipper, they'd sleep easily on this trans-Atlantic flight far above a stormy ocean.

"Among our passengers is a distinguished scientist, Allan Mezley, from Union College, upstate New York, on his way to Africa to study what he considers 'the most dangerous animal in Africa,' a snail that carries a disease called billariasis . . . or, as the British call it, 'Bill Harris.' This disease is a blood-fluke infection that, next to malaria, is the most widespread of all present-day tropical diseases. Patients afflicted with the disease feel lethargic and incapable of initiative."

And thus Lowell Thomas found, as he always does, fascinating topics and people close at hand.

To judge the wonders of the modern world one must, of course, be familiar with the glories of the old.

Lowell Thomas once told his son that he felt anything could be made exciting without stretching the truth—if you yourself were sufficiently interested. From childhood he had been fascinated by the stories he had read about the Seven Wonders of the World as the ancients reckoned them, and, on his own far travels, he had wondered, "What are the seven wonders of the modern world? Why not bring that ancient list up to date? Why not be the modern Antipater of Sidon who had named the seven Ancient Wonders?"

The idea took concrete form with Cinerama, and action was not far behind the idea. A long distance call between New York and London for Dr. Maynard Miller began with an enthusiastic greeting from a vibrant, familiar voice.

"Hello, Maynard. When are you coming back? . . . Would you like to go on a little jaunt for me? And, can you be ready to leave tomorrow?"

"To leave for where?" the doctor inquired.

"For a trip around the world," was the blithe reply.

The decision seemed sudden. Actually, the idea of filming the Seven Wonders of the World had been in the mind of Lowell Thomas for years. His studies had familiarized him with the facts of the once-accepted wonders to which travelers of 2,000 years ago flocked, just as tourists today journey to famous places. Ship captains and managers of camel caravans made profits in those days just as railways, ships and airlines make money today.

The original list had been made in the Alexandrian

period when the great city at the mouth of the Nile, founded by Alexander the Great, became the center of western civilization. Sightseeing was the vogue in the period between the glory of Greece and the fall of the Roman Empire.

The actual trip just to make plans for filming the seven wonders of the modern world, starting where the Greeks of antiquity had left off, still lay ahead. Now where to start on such a project? The crew for Cinerama was already in Europe—and where, asked Lowell Thomas, could a better beginning be made than on Olympus, the home of the gods, Jupiter with his thunderbolts, Apollo with his golden lyre, and Aphrodite, goddess of love!

Seen from the air, Olympus was a mere plateau, not even very craggy. But they, of course, also photographed the Acropolis, above Athens, crowned by the Parthenon. The Parthenon, unfortunately, was a mere skeleton of what it once had been. Only the columns with the architraves across their tops remained standing. Fragments of masonry lay about.

It was for Lowell Thomas to narrate the story of how the Parthenon was constructed by Pericles, as a temple to the goddess Athena. After the triumph of Christianity, for a time it became a church. When the Turks conquered Greece, the church became a mosque. Although roofless, the Parthenon remained intact until the tragedy came in the year 1687 A.D.

There had been attempts to expel the Turks from Greece by the Republic of Venice. Success was only temporary. The Venetian commander was an Admiral

Morosini, a sea hero of his day. After his troops had occupied Sparta and the Peloponnesus, Morosini was ready to attack the Greeks in Athens.

The Acropolis, on which the Parthenon stood, was a rocky hill. The citadel of Athens for centuries had been a natural stronghold for defense; the Turks used it as a fortress against the Venetians. They even had a gunpowder magazine in the Parthenon.

Whether or not Morosini knew of that gunpowder magazine is problematical. But this was war and he bombarded the Turks—in the Parthenon. A shell struck the gunpowder magazine. It exploded. The explosion shattered the walls and demolished the interior. All that was left standing were the columns with the architraves, fallen masses of masonry and masterpieces of sculpture.

When Morosini, upon capturing Athens, beheld the wreckage, the joy of his victory turned to grief. He was a man of culture who had been brought up on Tintoretto, Veronese, and Titian, and from childhood had been taught to venerate art in painting and sculpture.

He exclaimed brokenly, "O Athens, O Nursery of the arts! To what hast thou come?"

Tenderly he attempted to salvage some of the finer pieces, calling in willing soldiers. But their unskillful attempt resulted merely in mishandling. And so they returned home, leaving behind the precious wreckage.

It was not until the beginning of the 19th century that the British ambassador to Constantinople, Lord

Elgin, made an agreement with the Sultan to obtain the right to remove sculptured marble from the wreckage of the Parthenon in order to save it. And so it is that today the Elgin Marbles, much of the frieze from the Parthenon, may be viewed in the British Museum. They are regarded as one of the world's greatest art treasures, saved by a British diplomat.

Even what remains of the Parthenon must be reckoned one of the modern world's wonders. So why was it not included among the Seven Wonders of the Ancient World? It stood there in its pristine glory for all the world to see when the selections were made.

The only reason seems to be that it was not nearly as vast in size as that wonder of Asia Minor, the Temple of Diana at Ephesus. Everything chosen was colossal. The Parthenon was of classic moderation, restrained and with its frieze by Phidias.

Besides the Parthenon, Lowell Thomas instructed Paul Mantz to fly the Cinerama crew around the Leaning Tower of Pisa in Italy, an architectural curiosity that every tourist goes to see. It is 179 feet high and a gem, but tilts so far over that onlookers wonder how it stands up. It was erected in the 13th century as the bell tower, the campanile of the cathedral. There are many bell towers in Italy, but the one at Pisa draws most attention because, why does it lean? It was built on an insecure foundation and began to lean at an early date. A century ago it was fifteen and a half feet off the perpendicular. Today it is sixteen and a half feet. Perhaps that is the way it will remain, for modern engineering is employed to keep the Leaning Tower from toppling over.

Vesuvius had been a sleeping giant of a volcano for centuries until in the year 79 A.D. it erupted following a series of earthquakes. The two cities below, Pompeii and Herculaneum, were overwhelmed with lava and volcanic ash. Many perished. Pliny, investigating the tragedy, was overcome by the volcanic fumes and died.

Excavations extending over many years have amounted almost to a restoration. Lowell Thomas desired to show the resurrected cities as among the modern wonders of the world.

Flying along the coast of Normandy, Paul Mantz took pictures of a Gothic monastery that the Normans built of granite. It served as both a monastery and a fortress. They called it Mont St. Michel after the archangel with the fiery sword.

All over Europe and all over the world, the search continued.

Chapter Eight

In the Eternal City

Lowell Thomas had spent much time in Rome, the eternal city, a city with its ruins of ancient, medieval, and Renaissance days. Although today the visitor finds a modern metropolis, he is ever aware of the days of the Caesars, the art of the Renaissance, and the imprint of the Popes of the Middle Ages.

It was fortunate for Cinerama that the time chosen by Lowell Thomas for recording the Wonders of the Modern World coincided with that of an outstanding event. The Roman Catholic Church was celebrating the Marian Year, honoring the Virgin Mother with superb ritual.

Cinerama cameras to begin with, naturally picked out the biggest and best known ruins that history students associate with Rome—the Colosseum. Viewing the familiar site, the men remembered reading that here, in the heart of Rome, Nero had built a sumptuous palace for himself, the Golden House, with spacious gardens. The Golden House was torn down, and in its place the Emperor Vespasian and Titus erected the great amphitheater that could seat between forty and fifty thousand spectators. It was a place of savage sport. During the reign of the Emperor Trajan five thousand pairs of gladiators fought to the death, and it was here that Christians were thrown to the lions.

From the air the Colosseum looked to the Cinerama cameramen like a huge saucer. After all the long years, much of the massive structure is still standing, one of the most durable relics of the days when Rome ruled the world. There are few places that so attract students the world over. Even the most meagerly informed scholar knows that most gladiators were prisoners of war, condemned criminals, slaves. Yet there were free men, too, who volunteered for the glory of fighting in the arena before the Emperor and the people of Rome.

A champion gladiator was a popular hero, hailed, feted, the prize ring champion or astronaut of today. For the Christian martyrs to be thrown to the lions was, at the time, a legal mode of execution. Condemned criminals were given over to hungry beasts for a public death to afford entertainment for the public.

The gladiatorial fights were struggles to the death and were so cruel and bloody as to defy description. The general public not only enjoyed such spectacles, but it was fashionable to attend, just as prize fights and bull fights today are attended. These contests were shows to keep the public happy.

One single man stopped gladiatorial contests for all time. One day, during a bloody combat, a young boy's fair hair was matted with blood, his blue eyes half blinded, while his adversary continued to rain blows upon his head. A Christian monk leaped into the arena. He pushed between the gladiators, his arms upraised to heaven and demanded that in the name of Christian morality, the bloody, uneven fight cease.

"In God's name, I forbid this savage spectacle!" he shouted.

The enraged crowd swarmed down on him and set upon him with fists and swords and bludgeons. He was killed as he must have known he would be.

However, the reaction was strange. The martyr had not died in vain. An imperial decree abolished forever the spectacle of the gladiators.

But the Colosseum remained. True, in the Middle Ages robber barons used it as a quarry from which to obtain stones for their palaces. Yet in spite of such thefts, much of it has remained and is one of the wonders of ancient Rome that continues to lure tourists from all over the world.

Nearby, the camera sought out the Roman Forum with its graceful arches and columns. It must have been glorious at one time and one could easily visualize the processions of men in armor on horseback approaching it from the Appian Way and passing through its triumphal arches. It was easy, too, to envision the Senate House where Cicero and Caesar debated. The Roman Senate was an august governing body.

The open space of the Forum was even more important than the building. Here was the meeting place of the Assembly of the people. The space was equal to a city block and one can well imagine the mass of citizens gathered to vote on the enactment of laws and to elect public officials, the consuls, praetors, and aediles. The Assembly was legally the final authority; the Senate assumed the administration.

The Roman Forum is in no wise as well preserved as the Colosseum. But the laws made here shook the world from Mesopotamia to the Atlantic. A population of millions involving many great cities was affected.

Rome began as a city state, and the Forum was the market place. This republican government worked satisfactorily within that city state. But when Rome expanded into an empire, it failed, for the reason that the people of antiquity never devised a representative government. The Roman Empire was a type of monarchy, a man-made government.

Now was the supreme moment for the Cinerama camera to roam over the city and come to pause over St. Peter's Cathedral. This was 1956, the Marian Year. St. Peter's Cathedral was more than an architectural wonder. It was the largest and most beautiful church in the world. The majestic dome with Michelangelo's angels surely must be accepted as one of the stately wonders of the world.

The ceremonies of the Marian Year were moving to a close in a blaze of glory—a papal procession and a blessing by Pope Pius XII for the vast throng in the square of the cathedral.

Now was the momentous moment to be recorded in picture and sound for all the world to share.

Could it be done?

Back in New York Lowell Thomas had asked the aid of Cardinal Spellman to film the celebration of the Marian Year for the vast Cinerama screen. Cardinal Spellman obligingly wrote to the proper authorities at the papal court.

Lowell Thomas said, "But I wonder if he ever guessed how much we would ask for in Rome."

The interior of St. Peter's provided an appropriate setting for the brilliant pageantry of traditional Catholic ceremonies. Never before had the interior been lighted for films, but Lowell Thomas was determined to get close-ups, even intimate scenes, of the Pope during a papal procession as well as at Castel Gandolfo, the summer residence of the Pontiff outside Rome.

Becoming more ambitious to present St. Peter's in a light that would appeal to all ages and types of persons, Mr. Thomas suggested some light relief from the majestic ceremonies—a simple appealing story, perhaps.

No sooner was this idea expressed than the British playwright, William Lipscomb, who had helped George Bernard Shaw in the theater, set in motion a plan for a tale that had both pathos and comedy.

The story centered about a funny Giovanni and his wife, Maria, whose sick child had been almost magically restored to health. So grateful were the parents that they decided to take him to the celebration at St. Peter's, there to receive the papal blessing. Lipscomb, a genius at suspense, contrived various misadventures that resulted in delays so that the eager little family arrived too late for the ceremony. They could only offer a prayer at the high altar of the empty cathedral.

But all was not lost! Told that the Pope had gone to Castel Gandolfo where he is to give a special blessing, they hurry on. Again they almost miss out but finally make it. Their faces are radiant as they receive the blessing. William Lipscomb's reactions as a top film writer to what he considered Lowell Thomas' impossible plans for Rome are best expressed in his own words.

"When I first joined that strange collection of odd souls known as the Cinerama unit in Rome in November 1954, I thought they seemed the nicest bunch of thugs I had been mixed up with for a long time," he observed. "When it was explained that the idea was to shoot the interior of St. Peter's with lights and a sound truck whilst the service was going on, I knew they were mad and what they expected was impossible. But I was delighted that there were people in search of the Holy Grail.

"When they explained that they also wanted a close-up of the Pope himself giving a blessing, I knew they were indeed mad. As my old mother used to say, 'What will they think of next?' Americans think up the nicest ideas even though they seem impossible in practice. The picture in my mind was that of his Holiness being confronted with a camera that weighed about two thirds of a ton and his being asked to watch for the dickey bird. It sounded pleasantly fantastic.

"But it happened. Whilst I was saying it couldn't

be done, the great event—the impossible—took place. The next thing I knew we combed Italy for all the lights in the country, installed them right in St. Peter's church, arranged for generators and goodness knows what else, and there, with a full congregation of about fifty thousand people, was our strange band of technicians, lights, sound equipment, recording for the first time in history a service at St. Peter's . . . the chief ceremony of the Marian Year.

"There still remained that close-up of the Pope. I never thought they'd ever get that. But they did, and at his private residence at Gandolfo, on the hilltop. In the little square a scaffold about twenty feet high was erected just opposite the little balcony on which the Pope comes to give a special blessing to the few who obtain permission. It must have been astonishing for the little crowd of about a hundred who had come for the blessing—astonishing to find a platform twenty feet high, with a dozen sweating technicians led by the busiest cameraman in all the world, Harry Squire.

"But if the crowd was astonished, it was nothing to the amazement of the Pope himself. After all, he was coming out on the balcony to give his blessing as he had done a thousand times before. When he came out this time, he found himself confronted with a monstrous camera weighing about fifteen hundred-weight and looking something like a space ship. It was such a shock that he even hesitated over the blessing.

"Harry Squire, perfectionist that he was, could hardly ask a Pope for a retake. But, fortunately, the Pope himself is a perfectionist. He went back into his room and told his staff that he didn't think that was very satisfactory. Could he do it again? And so he came out once more and performed the blessing of the crowd all over again—a magnificent, austere figure indeed.

"I had been fiddling around with the story of the little family trying to get to St. Peter's for the blessing and being delayed everywhere. Now the tale of the little pilgrims could come to a happy ending."

It took Dr. Maynard Malcolm Miller, who for years had been leading expeditions to the mountains and glaciers in Alaska, to persuade the Vatican authorities to agree to the Cinerama proceedings. It was all the more difficult, for Pope Pius was just recovering from a severe illness.

Dr. Miller faced all the technical difficulties too. He reported, "St. Peter's is the largest single room in the world. We knew it would need whole banks of lights. . . . Filming required about seventy huge lights and a number of smaller ones. The Cinerama group had to hire sixteen large generators to be set up on each side of the basilica outside. Then there were the thousands of feet of cable strung through the burial vaults and along hidden passageways underneath the main part of St. Peter's in order to place the lights at strategic places. A series of ten to twenty-foot scaffolds had to be built for each set of lights. Because of religious ceremonies constantly taking place, the men could not work during these periods. But somehow sufficient lighting was put up by working right up to within an hour before the ceremony began. . . . The pictures of the interior of St. Peter's were brilliant. At Castel Gandolfo they were equally impressive."

Harry Squire, cameraman, gives a clear account of the photography done at St. Peter's.

"The Pope was to give his blessing from a balcony. The front of the balcony was enclosed by glass. For pictures made at close range, glints of light reflected into the camera lens. When the glass doors at the back were closed, reflected light interfered with the picture image. It was the custom to close the door, but the Pope was willing to make a concession.

"We secured Tom Conroy and Mike Mahoney to hold the door open. They were good Catholics and they were thrilled to meet the Pope and kiss his ring. . . . So that they wouldn't be seen by the cameras, they lay flat on the floor, holding the doors open. . . . In the picture you see the Pope close up as he blesses the crowd below, but he stops as if he were saying, 'Shall I give another blessing?' Actually, he's talking to Conroy and Mahoney on the floor. He speaks good English and he's asking them should he do it over. They say yes . . I'd have killed them if they didn't. So, his Holiness comes out and does a repeat. You'll see it in the pictures."

Later the Pope remarked, "Americans always want to be sure."

He was so pleased about it all that he gave Dr. Miller silver medals for the camera crew.

The beauty and color and artistry were unforgettable. The uniforms of the Swiss Guards at Castel Gandolfo had been designed by Michelangelo and are still the most famous uniforms in the world.

St. Peter's, the workers knew, represents the greatest architectural achievement of the Renaissance. The list of architects who presided over its creation is studded with great names like jewels in a crown: Bramante, Italian architect; Raphael, Italian painter; Michelangelo, the great Italian sculptor, painter, and architect; and Bernine who designed the superb colonnades.

This magnificent edifice, St. Peter's Cathedral, is, by any standards, a wonder of the modern world. And the way it was filmed, declared Lowell Thomas, was something of a wonder too.

Chapter Nine

A Missionary and a Dancer

Of one thing the Cinerama crew was certain. Africa, that vast plateau split by the Rift Valley, was bound to be a place of superlatives. The Dead Sea was the lowest body of water on earth. The Red Sea was part of the Rift Valley, and Lake Tanganyika was one of the largest fresh water lakes in the world. In the Mountains of the Moon were to be found many dead and sleeping volcanoes and some live ones too.

Lowell Thomas had a ground crew as well as a unit for aerial photography in the Cinerama group. Paul Mantz planned to get air shots of Kilimanjaro, Africa's loftiest peak, but he was prevented by cloudy weather. However, he spotted a live crater from the air and, in devil-dare fashion, dived for a picture. It was a dangerous stunt but he was rewarded with one of the most incredibly beautiful pictures ever made, a picture of a mirror lake in a remote African volcano crater.

In Rhodesia, the rocks in a plateau had cracked open to leave a canyon more than four hundred feet deep, as narrow as eighty feet but forty miles long.

Above this deep cleft, and flowing across the plateau placidly was the wide Zambezi River. The chasm cut straight across its path. The oncoming river, widest at this point, had no choice but to plunge over the edge of the canyon.

That plunging river is known as Victoria Falls. The river tumbles over one cliff and against another, then shoots down one canyon wall, only to strike against the opposite canyon wall.

The Cinerama crew was thrilled to be on the scene where the strange events had transpired. One and all, they relived that famous meeting, in which Stanley, after months of peril, found the long-missing explorer and said, "Dr. Livingstone, I presume," which Lowell Thomas calls "the height of British imperturbability and understatement."

The Cinerama cameras found plenty of wildlife in Africa, the lion, the leopard, the elephant, the rhinoceros, the hippopotamus, the giraffe and the antelope. Their film caught herds of galloping hippos or river horses, clouds of pink flamingos and countless crocodiles slithering on muddy riverbanks.

But the members of the camera crew found their greatest delight in filming a school for elephants in the Belgian Congo.

They watched the capture of a baby elephant from a wild herd. The tribesmen used trained elephants to isolate the calf from its mother. The old bull of the herd trumpeted in protest.

The school, outside the village, receives the new

pupil, tethering him to a stake. The baby is made to kneel and rise when the command is given; he receives a banana for good behavior. At the close of the day's work, the trainers ride the elephants in procession, singing a song. The training is gentle and kind, and the baby elephant soon learns to welcome the master who provides his food.

Lowell Thomas tells us that Hannibal's elephants were African, and much harder to train than the elephants of Asia. They carried castles on their backs from which archers shot arrows. They were a formidable enemy, especially when they charged, trampling down hostile soldiers. But being used to the jungles and the heat, many perished in the frigid weather of northern Italy.

Lowell Thomas wanted Cinerama to visit the Watusi of East Africa, the tallest people in the world. They live on the eastern border of the Belgian Congo near the greatest of the Rift Valley lakes, Tanganyika. Scientists cannot explain them. They are an anthropological wonder.

Arrangements for filming the Watusi had to be made with their king, scion of a dynasty that could trace back eighteen generations. His name, Charles Mutara II Rudahigwas. His subjects called him the Mwami.

He was about forty years old, somber in mien, lean, handsome —and six feet nine.

Bill Lipscomb dealt with the Mwami for Cinerama. This is his report to Lowell Thomas:

"One has preconceived notions of places. To me the Congo suggested Livingstone and miles of bearers carrying things on their heads. **All wrong.** Usumbura is a small town of new buildings, four-lane highways, good cafes and restaurants where you can eat as well as one can in Brussels. The Belgian banks are marble halls, and instead of natives carrying burdens on their heads, they carry them inside their heads and work adding machines. Even the post office is a beautiful pillared hall with politeness and attention thrown in.

"However, my business is with the king of the Watusi warriors, the Tall Men of Africa. So the king graciously receives me. He drives up in his sports Studebaker, gets out. He is nearly seven feet; he is dressed in perfect English tweeds. He speaks in perfect French. Who's embarrassed? I am, with my fourth grade French.

" 'Our dances,' he tells me, 'are traditional—like your square dances, or even your Maypole dances! But they do not reflect our life today. We are modern. All Africa is going modern.'

"And, charming though he was, he had the look that all Africans have in the back of their eyes—the question: 'When are you Europeans going to get the hell out of here and leave us to manage our own affairs?' "

The Mwami appeared in the Cinerama picture garbed in the traditional costume of the Watusi with royal robe and tribal ornaments, a truly regal figure. He dwarfed his Belgian adviser—made him look runtish and commonplace.

The Watusi of the Ruanda country are an artistocracy, and they demand all honors due. The local people are Bantus of ordinary stature, peasants who cultivate the land. The Watusi are indolent and lordly, proud of their high jumping and dancing.

With amazement the Cinerama crew watched the exhibition for Cinerama as the Watusi athletes went over the bar at more than seven feet. As an aid, the athlete would place one foot on a take-off stone before vaulting. As they performed, their monkey tails in their headdresses bobbed madly and the bells on their ankles jingled.

Among the many dancers there was a supreme artist. His name was Butera, the Nijinsky of the tribe. John Gunther best describes him:

"The leading dancer, by name Butera, seven feet five inches tall, weighs something like three hundred pounds. He is so celebrated as a dancer and high jumper, and so typical of the old Watusi, that his portrait appears on the local bank notes."

Gunther summarizes the situation when he says, "Yesterday kisses tomorrow."

Although the Watusi are coal black, they are not negroid. They are of a Hametic race and are thought to have come down from the north. Even anthropologists cannot account for their excessive stature. But Bill Lipscomb got an explanation from the Mwami himself.

"He told me the royal 'joke,'" says Bill. "It's his own joke and it is told with proper dignity.

"Why are all Watusi so tall? Because, when you are very young, your father boots you in the behind every morning to make you jump. So you jump and you grow tall!"

It is a very little joke, but it's the King's own and therefore very laughable.

Lowell Thomas saw, in these strange, tall, black men, interesting and likeable human beings, whom he featured in colorful, dramatic pictures for his Cinerama.

Chapter Ten

The Holy Land

Lowell Thomas knew that he faced a big problem in handling the story of Palestine, especially difficult in view of the tension between Israel and the Arabs. It was decided to cut the picture into two natural sequences, the Old Testament and the New Testament. Events were to move in chronological order, the first part in Exodus showing a sequence of places in the progress of the children of Israel. The second part would begin at Bethlehem and carry the Gospel story.

The scenes would give plenty of scope, and the narrating of the greatest story ever told would be handled by Lowell Thomas himself, using the King James version of the Bible, a clear advantage.

The musical background was a challenge but it was ably handled by Emil Newman who worked in collaboration with Jerome Moross. The symphonic effect was produced for the Biblical themes, giving the movement great dignity and beauty.

The action began in the land of Goshen, as seemed most logical. When Herod ordered the slaying of the

Israelite sons, Moses' Hebrew mother placed her baby in an ark in the bulrushes. Here in the reeds along the Nile the daughter of the Pharaoh found him and took him to the palace where he was nurtured in royal style.

The narrative accompanying this part of the picture is taken from Exodus. Moses again and again repeated to the Pharaoh the command of the Lord: "Let my people go!"

The music, like a Hebrew chant, rises in a chorus of voices, pleading and commanding.

Mount Sinai must needs come into the picture. It is just outside Egypt, beyond Suez. Here is the mountain of the Ten Commandments. It is steep, jagged, formidable.

Lowell Thomas' rich tones do the narration:

"And it came to pass, when the people heard the sounds of the trumpet, and the people shouted with a great shout, that the wall fell down flat."

Now the road is seen again, leading from Jericho to Jerusalem.

Cinerama photographed the entrance to Jerusalem by St. Stephen's Gate. Here the first Christian martyr was stoned to death.

Nazareth, like Jerusalem and Bethlehem, became part of the Cinerama scene, for here it was that Jesus grew to manhood in the carpenter's home of Joseph and Mary.

The Cinerama crew did some beautiful photography of the Sea of Galilee with its pleasant shores. Being set deep among rugged hills, it was naturally subject to storms. It was here that Jesus walked on the water.

On the banks of the Jordan where John the Baptist, "The Voice in the Wilderness," baptized Jesus, they shot outstanding pictures of the valley and its surroundings, and overlooking the Jordan, the Mount of Temptation, where Jesus was tempted by Satan.

The Cinerama camera caught not only the craggy valley of the Jordan, but the still beauty of the Sea of Galilee, so reminiscent of the psalm, "He leadeth me beside the still waters."

The tremendous Christian tragedy is presented with the background of historic scenes with proper Bible narration. The imagination enacts the scenes of sorrow and suffering, and supplies the persons.

"Then cometh Jesus with them to a place called Gethsemane" and here is recalled the agony in the Garden.

Now the camera again depicts St. Stephan's Gate and follows events along the "Via Dolorosa," the Way of the Cross, named by tradition as the road to Calvary.

The final scenes are scenes of triumph over death. At the Church of the Holy Sepulchre the scene of the Resurrection is recalled. Here, on every Easter, the cry rings out, "He is risen! He is risen!" and it is echoed in every church in Christendom.

The Cinerama camera caught the Mount of Olives, the scene of the Ascension, and here one of those fortuitous accidents happened that resulted in a glorious effect.

For background they needed some cloud shots. The two photographers consulted and Harvey Manger looked up a few. He found a scene that had been discarded as defective. It was a shot of a sea of gleaming clouds made from an airplane. However, light had glinted into the lens.

"Halation," the film men call it, from the word "halo." There were streaks of light from the top down the middle, and light streaks with branching streams of light.

Newman and Manger knew at once that they had something. The light streaks in the clouds might have been symbolism. It looked like a skillfully contrived effect to represent a mystical sign. It looked, in fact, like the Resurrection, and it would mean exactly that to any onlooker.

"How did you ever produce that optical effect in the cloud shot of the Ascension?" they were asked.

It was an inspired accident, but it was glorious in its result.

Lowell Thomas had spared no pains to get the inspiring musical effect for this scene. The designed magnificence was produced through his friends of the Apollo Club of Minneapolis. This ensemble of male voices gave rich, resonant tone to the climax of the greatest story ever told.

There remained the job of assembling the picture that was to be produced as Cinerama.

An epilogue was planned, a montage depicting familiar American wonders like Niagara Falls and the Grand Canyon.

All the wonders of the ancient world were of stone. How about structural steel as building material that could outlast the centuries? Take the Empire State, the tallest building in the world.

Anybody who has ever been to New York City has seen the Empire State building and will be interested in its history. In 1799 the land on which it stands was a farm owned by John Thompson. When he offered to sell it for $7,000 he published a "for sale" sign which read, "The rapid growth of the city and the village of Greenwich and Chelsea will cause the value of this property to be greatly enhanced."

As Lowell Thomas says, "John should see it now!"

The seven wonders of the Ancient World were monumental, religious, or aesthetic. Only one, the Pharos, the lighthouse of Alexandria, was utilitarian. The modern world's wonders are chiefly utilitarian steel bridges, the Hoover dam, modern highways, jet aviation.

Standing out from all the technological marvels is a little white church, his own church in the Berkshire Hills of eastern New York, symbol of the Protestant faith. It is eloquent of Puritan tradition and was photographed as such by Cinerama.

In all the world nothing is more spectacular than our own Grand Canyon, 280 miles long, four to eighteen miles wide and more than a mile deep. The sculptor that produced those fantastic cliffs and pinnacles was the Colorado River. The colorings are some of the most fantastic that the human eye can behold.

Niagara Falls, which dates back only to the ice age, is spectacular in beauty, a favorite resort for honeymooners. It is sometimes called the sentimental wonder of the world.

The American sequence for Cinerama ends with the redwoods of California. The sequoia, as the Cinerama crew realized, is the largest and tallest of trees and the oldest of living things. Some of the sequoias are more than three thousand years old and were standing when pharaohs of the line of Rameses were reigning in Egypt. All visitors admire General Sherman, 300 feet high, with a base of a hundred and one feet.

Lowell Thomas reports, "We took the 3-eyed camera for a ride through the redwoods of Yosemite. The peripheral vision makes it seem as if the trees and foliage are brushing past you. With brilliance of light and shade among the towering sequoias, the effect is dazzling and comes to a close with a gasp, as you approach a precipice and seem about to go over but remain gazing over a glorious valley."

What an inspiring ending for Cinerama, with this view of our own America!

Chapter Eleven

The Land of the Pyramids and the Sphinx

In Cinerama's search for the Wonders of the World, the photographers found only one ancient wonder that had survived up to the present day. Lowell described it as "monstrosities in stone" and he referred, of course, to the pyramids of Egypt and the Sphinx. He was reminded of the tourist who reasoned, "I suppose the Sphinx must have been built by a Mister Sphinx."

It was on his way from Italy to Palestine that Lowell Thomas first beheld the Pyramids. His main objective at the time was to cover General Allenby's campaign to conquer the Holy Land by driving out the Turks. Seeing the Pyramids was purely incidental. He stopped off in Egypt like any traveler and took off from a military field at ancient Heliopolis with a Royal Flying Corps flier in a fighter plane. To show his guest the Pyramids and the Sphinx, he would dive down at them.

Lowell Thomas recounts the incident: "With the Pyramids and the Sphinx coming up at me, it looked as if we'd crash into the apex of the Pyramid of Cheops. But the plane leveled off and circled around for a more leisurely view. The impression I still retain is of the Pyramids and the Sphinx coming up at me."

Soon he was to have another look. Wishing to join Lawrence of Arabia later, he learned that he could not go directly to Lawrence's headquarters in the desert near the head of the Gulf of Akaba because he would have had to go through the Turkish lines in disguise. He was compelled to make a circuitous journey, and this enforced detour took him to Egypt again, up the Nile to the Sudan, across the Red Sea by boat to Jedda and finally north to the port of Akaba.

It was while he was in Cairo on this journey that he decided to have another look at the Pyramids. He had no desire for another wild flight. Accordingly, he joined a party of British soldiers who were sightseeing. A lorry took them to Gizeh where camels were provided for the rest of the trip.

Years later the Cinerama cameras caught the same scene. The crew came out from Cairo just as he had. Through the miracle of motion pictures the existence of the only surviving wonder of the ancient world was recorded for the vast new screen, and Lowell Thomas spoke the lines that accompanied the scenes when shown to the world.

He knew that even the Greeks of antiquity esteemed the Pyramids of Egypt as the greatest and oldest of the Seven Wonders. In their day great mystery surrounded them.

Pliny, the authority on the subject, wrote, "We must make mention of the Pyramids of Egypt, idle and frivolous pieces of ostentation on the part of the mon-

Count Felix von Luckner and Lowell Thomas, 1962

Lowell Thomas, the skier

Lowell Thomas with two ski companions in the High Sierras. The one on the left, a member of the first American Women's Olympic Team.

Lowell Thomas, the skier

archs of that country. Indeed, it is asserted by most persons that the only motive for constructing them was either a determination not to leave their treasures to their successors or to rivals that might be plotting to supplant them, or to prevent the lower classes from remaining unoccupied. There was great vanity displayed by these men in constructions of this description."

The present view is most logical. The labor force consisted of the peasant population in the off season, when the Nile flood was on and there was nothing to do while the fields were inundated. This, Lowell Thomas thinks, is the real answer to the question, "Who did the actual labor of building the Pyramids of Egypt?"

Pliny's opinion that the Pyramids were mere "idle and frivolous pieces of ostentation" does not hold water either. They were not mere vanity, as we know now they were the tombs of the Pharaohs of the Fourth Dynasty. Their purpose was to insure, in a gigantic way, the welfare of the king in the future life. The material luxuries would have their spiritual counterpart in the world beyond the tomb.

Pliny asserted that the Pyramids were surrounded by desert sand, with no buildings of any sort. That was the way Lowell Thomas saw them. That is the way the visitor will see them today.

But archaeologists tell a different story.

There had once been elaborate buildings extending to the neighboring hills. These shrines and other edifices of the cult of the royal deceased were part of the plan to serve the royal mummy as he had been served in life. Numerous priests carried on a ritualistic worship. They served beside the magnificent sarcophagi in which their Pharaohs slept the sleep of death.

As among the American Indians, the Pharaohs in their pyramid tombs were surrounded by objects such as they used in life. It was thought that these appurtenances were necessary for the future life.

Lowell Thomas actually saw one of the far-famed "solar boats" that had been designed to carry a Pharaoh on his celestial journey to the Sun god. The boat had been discovered by a party of archaeologists just at the time the Cinerama crew had arrived at the Pyramids. It was a typical Nile boat, the type shown in ancient Egyptian drawings.

This particular burial place had been looted even to the mummy, but the boat was there after five thousand years.

Much has been learned since Pliny gave out what he considered facts. He probably knew about the religious belief of the Egyptian, that each man had a sort of shadow of self, his **ka**—that every one of his possessions also had a shadow reality. What he did not know were the facts read from the hieroglyphic inscriptions interpreted by archaeologists.

The great Pyramid, they learned, was built by Khufu, whom the Greeks called Cheops. The second was constructed under Khafra. The third and smallest was built by the Pharaoh Menhaura of Gizeh.

Pliny did give a vivid pictorial view of the wonder. His Egyptian wonders are clearly described.

He said, "In front of these pyramids is the Sphinx, a still more wondrous object of art, but one upon which silence has been observed as it is looked upon as a divinity by the people of the neighborhood. It was hewn from the solid rock; and, from a feeling of veneration the face of the monster is colored red."

The sphinx that Lowell Thomas and the Cinerama crew saw showed no trace of red. Doubtless the weather had washed that strange head. Nor was there any mystery or silence over the desert.

Hieroglyphic inscriptions reveal, Lowell Thomas reports, that the Sphinx at Gizeh represented the Sun god Harmachis, on guard in the vicinity of the pyramid tombs.

According to Greek myth, a sphinx is a monster having a lion's body, wings, and the head and bust of a woman. The Sphinx of Thebes, according to legend, proposed a riddle to all passers. A wrong guess and they died! Oedipus guessed it, whereupon the Sphinx slew herself and he became king of Thebes.

What was the riddle, and what was the answer?

The riddle: What creature walks in the morning upon four feet, at noon upon two, at evening upon three?

The answer: MAN—as a baby on hands and knees, later on his feet, and in old age with a staff.

The Sphinx at Gizeh was that of a recumbent lion having the head of a man. The Sphinx at Gizeh represented Harmachis, the morning sun, a ram, or a hawk.

The Cinerama crew shot the Pyramids and the Sphinx in the hot desert sun. And for Lowell Thomas this wonder of the ancient world still remained a wonder of the modern world. After two thousand years he felt that list of Seven Wonders should be brought up to date. So, with his big private DC-6 airliner that he called the "Cinerama Clipper," he flew on around the world in search of wonders.

Chapter Twelve

Land of Gold, Frankincense, and Myrrh

From the Pyramids and the Sphinx Lowell Thomas and crew flew on to nearby lands that had supplied the Pharaohs of Egypt with the luxuries they demanded. In those days, one neighbor was Arabia Felix, Arabia the Blessed. For centuries the kingdom of Saba was the richest and most powerful state in all Araby, rich and tropical in contrast to the unproductive desert sands that lay so near.

Saba's wealth was due to her ability to produce and export aromatic frankincense, myrrh, cinnamon, and cassia. The demand was limitless, for the ancients prized these products for their religious ceremonials and for the preparation of fragrant unguents, perfumes, and medicinal ointments. Spices were also much used in cooking and preservation.

Not only did the Sabeans ship out, by camel caravan and by boat, these precious aromatic substances to Egypt, Palestine, and Syria, but they also dealt in gold and precious stones, including pearls.

Lowell Thomas knew that there was no such luxury today in southern Arabia, the Yemen or the Hadramaut. Modern life had changed the complexion of Arabia Felix. Nevertheless, in the big Cinerama Clipper, he and his crew flew from a field near Cairo for an air journey down the Red Sea to Aden. Here is his report on this by tape:

"Last night we took off from the airfield at Heliopolis, bound for South Arabia, the part of Arabia that the Romans called Arabia Felix, Arabia the Blessed, the land of the Queen of Sheba, ancient land of frankincense and myrrh. At Heliopolis I remembered that in the days of the Pharaohs here was located the University of Ahn (On) which Moses is said to have attended. . . . Crossing the southern end of the Suez Canal, we flew over the Red Sea right about where the Israelites made that fabulous crossing on dry land, and then on past Mount Sinai where Moses went up to the mountain top and received the Ten Commandments from Jehovah. . . . Then on through the night we flew through a sky full of stars, shining only as stars can shine over the Arabian desert. Skirting the Hejaz, the part of Arabia that includes the two most sacred and forbidden Moslem cities, Mecca and Medina, we swept on south, past the Yemen, a closed country over which no airplanes are supposed to fly except those owned by the king.

"To the right of the Cinerama Clipper lay the African coast of Eritrea and French Somaliland. Below us the Strait of Bab el Mandeb. Rounding the cape that marks the south end of the Red Sea, from the cockpit we caught sight of a huge new British oil refinery at

Aden, built by my friend Steve Bechtel of San Francisco."

Lowell Thomas estimated the nonstop flight from Cairo as 1300 miles, and recalled from history how the Romans sent an army into this nearby Arabian desert only to suffer such losses through disease, fatigue, and famine that the expedition was called one of Rome's major military disasters. But the Cinerama party landed safe and fresh, and some hours later Lowell Thomas made another report:

"Aden, where I am tonight, is another of the world's faster growing cities. Aden has been an important trade center for some thousands of years. Although we don't know how long, we do know that the ships of the Pharaohs and of King Solomon came here. The present, however, may be the biggest boom period in Aden's history.

"With the British pulling out of Egypt, this city, more than one thousand miles to the south of Suez, here at the southern end of the Red Sea, has become the chief British port for this part of the world. In fact, the boom has been so swift that Aden almost overnight has jumped to the front as the third seaport in the British Commonwealth in tonnage of ships handled.

"Aden has a daily floating population of over a hundred thousand, mostly men. They sleep on string beds, Indian 'charpoys' which they rent. Just put them up anywhere in the streets at night, mostly in the section called The Crater, a desolate pocket surrounded by peaks that look like the mountains of the moon."

With that floating population of over a hundred thousand, there are, necessarily, many problems. Lowell Thomas points out three serious ones.

First of all, labor. On one occasion, when fifteen hundred Somalis were brought in from Africa as technicians to help out the Bechtel San Francisco engineering firms, eight thousand resentful Arabs attacked them. The fighting lasted all night, with a resulting four hundred casualties.

Along with the labor problem is the dope problem. A drug called Kat is flown in from Ethiopia. The workmen chew the leaves. Thus they gain a feeling of temporary courage and visions of bliss. The drug is habit-forming.

The third big problem has to do with race riots. Even though Aden is said to be the original Garden of Eden and the natives point out the tomb of Cain, the son of Adam and Eve who killed his brother Abel, it might well be thought that the land has the mark of Cain upon it. Most of the year the place is a fiery furnace. Surely there is nothing to suggest the cool beauty of a garden. Hatreds of races persist, with many fancied antagonisms.

However, many famous names remind both citizens and travelers of past glories. In the harbor at Aden there is the Queen of Sheba's Boat Yard. Here many boats lie at anchor or move out under sail. Scores of seagoing craft made of teakwood from the Malabar coast, and sturdily built dhows are frequent, filled with Arab produce.

On the land side, Lowell Thomas points out, there

is a small canyon leading from the mountains into Aden. This corridor of rocks they call King Solomon's Gate, through which trains of camels make their way as they come in from the desert.

To the north of Aden, in nearby Yemen, are the ruins of the ancient city of Marib, supposed to have been the Queen of Sheba's capital. Lowell Thomas asks, "Who was this legendary queen?"

The Bible tells this familiar story:

"And when the Queen of Sheba heard of the fame of Solomon concerning the name of the Lord, she came to prove him with hard questions.

"And she came to Jerusalem with a very great train, with camels that bore spices and very much gold and precious stones.

"And she gave the King a hundred and twenty talents of gold, and of spices very great store and precious stones: there came no more such abundance of spices as these which the Queen of Sheba gave to King Solomon."

Legend relates the Biblical account to the Kingdom of Saba, land of frankincense, and makes the Queen of Sheba a Sabean queen.

Actually, Lowell Thomas reasons, the Queen must have belonged to some lesser kingdom along the spice route. Much of such legend, he points out, comes from the Arabs whose Islamic religion is derived largely from the Bible.

The small wars in the wild regions north of Aden seldom reach the outside world to become news. Yemen is really a rich country in southwest Arabia. It has fabulous wealth, but the rulers want as little as possible to do with the outside world. Travelers are seldom welcomed. Indeed, the country is rarely visited by Westerners.

Yemen claims the thirty or forty south Arabian sultanates over which the British have a protectorate. The constant border wars make it tough for the British who continue their uncertain rule over this exotic region.

On the Red Sea coast of the Yemen lies the famous city of Mocha, a name that stands for the best in coffee.

The ancient kingdom of Saba may have had its frankincense and myrrh, but the modern principality of Yemen has its coffee—which is its gold.

For many years, Lowell Thomas reminds us, Mocha was the world's chief coffee port. Coffee is really native to Ethiopia where the coffee tree grows wild, but the original home of coffee cultivation was the Yemen.

The history of coffee is modern. Coffee has been identified with Arabia and Java, just as tea has been identified with the Chinese and with the island of Ceylon. Its use has spread since the founding of Islam. The Koran forbade coffee as an intoxicant, but every pious Moslem teacher drank it to keep awake during prolonged religious services.

Coffee was in vogue in Europe in the seventeenth century. An Austrian captive soldier, it is said, liked it and introduced it in Vienna. It spread to London and Paris where coffee houses became popular.

Shortly after Lowell Thomas and his Cinerama crew returned home, revolts broke out in the Yemen. Today, Lowell Thomas says, "Yemen has one of the most troubled governments on earth. But conditions may improve. Being opened to Western enterprises and business in oil, it may grow in prosperity and, hopefully, wisdom."

Chapter Thirteen

A Deep Dam in the Land of Frankincense

There did exist a Garden of Eden in Arabia at Marib. This fact was proved by two American achaeologists, Wendell Phillips and Professor William F. Albright of Johns Hopkins who excavated the ancient ruins of Yemen. Lowell Thomas, in searching out the wonders of the modern world, felt he must not overlook the site of the famous Marib Dam. The explorers had unearthed six hundred ancient pieces of alabaster before they were driven out. Resentful Arabs had no time for the newcomers.

But what they found was important. Lowell Thomas quotes Dr. Phillips who says, "Lying a few miles out from the old city, it is really a series of dam sections which are still standing. . . . We saw where whole sections of mountainside had been carved away alongside the dam to form spillways to irrigate the adjacent fields. The dam had served as the central control for the mass of waters pouring down from the mountains of Yemen, the spot from which it was distributed to create mile after mile of green fields.

"Most amazing was the way the large stone walls had been put together. Huge boulders were so perfectly dressed that they fitted into each other like pieces of a jigsaw puzzle, no trace of mortar in walls fifty feet high, standing as they had been when Sheba's great artisans built them about 2700 years ago."

Was the Marib Dam one of the world's wonders so long ago? What had become of it? Lowell Thomas had looked into the cause of its destruction and learned that a great cloudburst had destroyed the dam in the sixth century. He says, "There is hardly an historical event in pre-Islamic history that has become embellished so much with fanciful stories as the bursting of the Marib Dam."

The Koran relates this story: "The people of Sheba had beautiful gardens with good fruit. Then the people turned away from God, and, to punish them, He burst the dam, turning the good gardens into gardens bearing bitter fruit."

Actually, facts point out the real cause of the ruin of the Marib Dam. It was neglected as the trade routes at the beginning of the Christian era changed from the caravan trail to the sea route. In time, the much-neglected dam gave way, as do all neglected things.

The Cinerama crew had no chance to photograph the ruined dam, but some spectacular photography was in the offing.

Lowell Thomas decided to take a trip to Wadi Beihan to visit a sheik, and his crew took some fantastic pictures of the Rub' al Khali or the "Empty Quarter." Here is his report:

"I have just made a trip along what you could call the edge of the unknown, a flight across a country which has, for its eastern borders, the sand of the Rub' al Khali. That's the 'Empty Quarter.' "

For three hours he flew with two RAF flyers of Aden over barren mountains, then out into the great Arabian desert. For the first hour, he reports, the men flew at five to eight thousand feet so that the plane almost touched the jagged mountains of the Sultan of Zanzibar. It soared over other sultanates. The fortresses, the villages, and the towns were all perched on lofty peaks or knife-edge ridges. The flyers were aware that, for centuries, these people had raided each other and that every man carried a rifle or a curved sword. They had seen such armed men on the streets of Aden.

To live, they had to do some planting and some harvesting. In the narrow valleys below, Lowell Thomas and his flyers could see small fields of grain along with wild figs and tamarisk, which was supposed to yield a sort of manna. Oftentimes, the men had heard, these fields were raided by wild baboons. Living, from western standards, was indeed precarious.

Looking down, they saw Arabia as few people are privileged to see it, a country ringed by desolate mountains which enclose the blistering desert. The fortress villages rose here and there on the summits. And so ended the first hour.

During the second hour of the flight, as the plane soared inland, the land looked even drier, as though there were even less rainfall. Surely there were fewer villages. A wide valley appeared and it extended to the horizon. Could this be the Wadi Beihan, ruled over by the Sherif Hussein, the most important Arab ruler between the Aden sultanates and the Yemen? The sand dunes below were like a sea of sand rolling on forever and ever.

Below, the three men in the plane spotted a now familiar sight, the remains of the Marib Dam. Strange that once this site was an important city, the capital of the country ruled over by the fabled Queen of Sheba. Here stood an ancient Arabian metropolis boasting temples of marble and alabaster, dedicated to the Moon god.

Lowell Thomas describes his experience at this point:

"After circling the lost kingdom of Saba, with its half-excavated Moon temple on the sands below and the remains of the Marib Dam, the plane flew on in search of the ruler of the Wadi Beihan. Our Australian pilot had gotten lost on purpose in order to see the great ruins. Naturally, there was little chance for photography."

But nearby Wadi Beihan was to prove both picturesque and dramatic.

Wadi Beihan was an oasis with a town, a mud fort, and a rudimentary airstrip that has been built by the British. The Cinerama cameramen had arrived overland. They were a trifle pale from their reception, which was gunfire. However, it turned out that gunfire was merely a form of tribal salute. With the cameramen was Eileen Salama who had been with the Phillips archaeological party at Marib a couple of years before. She was an Egyptian who spoke Arabic as her mother tongue.

Lowell Thomas was much impressed by Sherif Hussein. He was of dignified bearing as became a ruler. Bearded, with rugged, handsome features, he looked what he was, an important potentate. Several sheiks from tribes out in the desert had come to pay their respects. Some merely kissed his hand. Others kissed not only his hand, but the dagger which he wore on his hip.

For entertainment of his special guests, Sherif Hussein decided on a camel stampede. It began with horsemen dashing forward, shooting guns. Then came the rush of camels. Lowell Thomas said, "It was a sight to see, a thousand camels charging straight at us, then veering off for a long procession. These camels were the wealth of Sherif Hussein."

The principal guest sat with the Sherif at the entrance of a handsome red tent. Inside the tent was the Cinerama camera. Harry Squire, in charge, kept his gaze on the camel stampede and also on the mud fort. On top stood vigilant guards, stationed there with machine guns.

The visitors were interested in the type of vegetation that grew in the broken desert country where spaces of open sand gave way to ridges and gullies. The gullies held the scant moisture enough so that brush and stunted trees and sparse grass might grow. There was no lush growth anywhere.

One certain tree was prized. It grew close to the

ground with the branches beginning almost at ground level and putting forth small leaves. The bark was gray. Yet this tree is the frankincense tree. Its sap was ancient treasure and it is still valuable today.

Methods of collecting frankincense have never, over the centuries, changed. A worker makes an incision in the bark of the tree. A greenish, sweet-smelling sap oozes out, forming a globule that hardens in the air. These globules are collected, and the cuts deepened for further oozing of sap. The hardened globules are packed in sheepskin or goatskin bags, making a precious cargo to go out along the caravan route.

A great deal of the aromatic products were sold in Egypt where they were burned in shrines or used in funerary rituals. In the Book of Nehemiah there is an account of a great chamber in Jerusalem where frankincense was stored along with other spices. The Gospel tells of the three Wise Men from the East bringing to the newborn Saviour gifts of gold and frankincense and myrrh.

The great Arabian physician, Avicenna, prescribed frankincense as a remedy for everything from tumors to fever, and in China it was considered a cure for leprosy.

While modern medicine insists that it has no curative properties, it is still being used in the Orient. The Hadramaut still exports a good deal to India where, in the temples, its fragrant clouds of smoke rise from the burning braziers.

Chapter Fourteen

The Skyscraper Cities of the Desert

Lowell Thomas had taken the lofty towers of New York City pretty much for granted. And he had been amazed at the tall many-storied palace of the Dalai Lama in Tibet. But he was totally unprepared for the skyscraper cities of the Hadramaut. True, he had heard of them, but actually seeing skyscrapers rising seemingly out of nowhere was a shock to this much-traveled man.

Following Sherif Hussein's show of onrushing camels, the Cinerama crew, with the Australian and New Zealand RAF pilots, flew towards the Arabian desert.

Lowell Thomas relates the experience: "We flew east and a little south of the only partially explored area where the British protectorate of Aden and the little known country of Yemen and the vast Rub' al Khali desert come together . . . An hour over the uninhabited desert, then above a waterless valley that was growing wider and deeper! This is the head of the Wadi Hadramaut.

"The valley resembles our Grand Canyon of the Colorado in Arizona, except that it is not so steep and the colors of the strata in the walls are not so brilliant. The color here in the Wadi Hadramaut is predominantly dark red.

"After flying for about an hour and a half from the eastern borders of the Yemen, we came to what are known as the four principal cities of the Hadramaut: Hauta, Shibam, Sciyan Tarim and Sciyum. These are the skyscraper cities! The most striking of the four: Shibam!

"When it suddenly appears around a cliff that juts out into the great red valley, you simply can't believe your eyes. For here is a city of some six hundred of these skyscrapers with streets between them like narrow canyons. The city is made up entirely of tall buildings. Most of them are dazzling white.

"The principal industries of the Wadi Hadramaut today are making yarn, weaving cloth, tanning hides, preparing indigo, and making the plaster that is used in the skyscrapers. But the chief export for centuries has been—young men. Around thirty per cent of their young men leave when they are in their teens. This situation demands an explanation. They go to the East Indies and Malaya where they enter the world of commerce. Ninety-five per cent of the Arabs in the Straits Settlements and Indonesia are Hadramis. They seem to have a flair for commerce. After ten or fifteen years they return, some of them bringing hundreds of thousands of dollars. Then they build more skyscrapers."

Actually, the skyscrapers that the Lowell Thomas

party beheld were only about eight stories high, but they looked much taller because they are unexpectedly there in the middle of the desert.

Today there is a new trend in the Hadramaut as in our own skyscraper cities. People long to get away from the city into the outskirts or into the country. The skyscraper city of Shibam is situated in the middle of the sun-baked desert but at an oasis with quite a bit of vegetation.

Before the days of the soaring planes, it was only birds that could look down upon these cities, birds off their course. But these cities had been found, though no one believed the stories of the tall cities, thinking these stories were merely tall tales.

The first European to write about them was a German named Von Werder. It is said that even in Texas, where the big story is usually acceptable, the listeners refused to accept Von Werder's tale as being too far out. They said in a supreme effort to prove the veracity of his tale, he despaired. He had no Cinerama camera, unfortunately.

Then an adventuresome Englishman named W. H. Ingrams rediscovered the skyscraper cities. They intrigued and delighted him. He became adviser to the Sultan of Mukalla and Shihr on the coast. Mukalla is a skyscraper seaport. It is located between Aden and where the Wadi Hadramaut enters the Indian Ocean.

Before the remarkable Ingrams came into the picture, life in the skyscraper cities was not entirely pleasant. True, rich Hadramis built new skyscrapers upon returning home as had their forebears. But they also got out their rifles and carried on endless feuds with their neighbors. Often they made slaves of their captives. It was quite common for families to keep slaves.

Soon after Ingrams started his work, the wealthy, more cultured families began to change their way of living. True, they still had their city homes, but they began to build villas in the country nearby. A date grove with shady palms made for real luxury.

The destructive tribal wars had caused endless harm and brought no happiness to anybody. Between 1934 and 1940 Ingrams persuaded the men to stop these senseless wars. Slavery was a harder reform to bring about. The Sultan of Mukalla did not free his slaves until 1944. For that matter, slavery still went on inland and does even to this day.

The Cinerama crew decided that the Islamic architecture they photographed would not look out of place in a Syrian or Egyptian setting. The craggy mesa below looked a lot like our own American southwest. Travel differed, of course. All the travel about the desert was by camel, for the camel's padded feet are best suited to desert sand.

With his three companions, Lowell Thomas buzzed the Sultan's gray, blue, and white palace at Seiyum. A car came out to pick up the callers who had just arrived by plane. And what a car! It was a 1929 Chevrolet that had been brought into the desert by camel caravan and assembled on the spot. In spite of age and tough usage, it still ran.

The natives and the guests were shown a documentary film that had been sent out by the British government. It was the first motion picture ever shown in Seiyum, and it showed Queen Elizabeth visiting Australia.

Lowell Thomas discovered that the population was divided into various classes and that there existed nothing that even resembled a democracy. Strangely enough, to the Cinerama crew, musicians and dancers were graded at the bottom of the lowest class.

The visitor would not soon forget the fine entertainment that was meted out to him and his men. He spent the night in the palace of a hundred rooms. Dinner was served with all the guests sitting on the floor on Persian rugs spread in the middle of a vast hall. Strange dishes were topped off with dates and pomegranates. Lowell Thomas confessed that he felt like a caliph of old until his knees creaked when he arose after the elaborate banquet.

The camera crew secured fine, clear pictures of the skyscraper cities of Shibam and Seiyum. The tall buildings are shown near an oasis where there is underground water. But where did all the people get their water in this desert country? Surely not many had homes on an oasis.

The cameramen soon learned that all the water used in the city came from a deep well. They went to watch a group of natives pulling a long rope, at a run. Thus a bucket of water is hauled up out of the well. The process goes on all day long with different shifts of workers.

Why, the cameramen wondered, did these south Arabians build skyscrapers in the first place? Why these tall buildings with the narrow canyons? It all grew out of tribal conditions. At first, in their earlier history, height offered a lookout for enemy raiders. Then it became the style. Besides, an Arab sheik explained, these buildings are warm in winter, for the winters are mild; and in the summer they are cool.

As for the people of the Hadramaut, where did they come from? Men do not choose desert country as a rule. The Arabs themselves say they are descendants of Shem, Noah's son. The term Semite is derived from this premise.

It has been noted by modern scholars that the earliest Egyptians were of the same physical type as the Arabians. So, it is possible that as the population in Egypt increased beyond the capacity of the ancient fertile land to support its people, some were forced into the nomadic life of the desert, to wander there with their sheep and camels. Eventually necessity and certainly a high degree of ingenuity combined to produce the skyscraper cities of southern Arabia.

Chapter Fifteen

The Rich Oil Men of the Desert

When Lowell Thomas found himself in Bahrein, he, of course, knew that he was at the focal center of the Middle East realm of oil, for some of his personal friends had played a part in developing the oil fields of the Middle East. Here were the headquarters of the largest oil fields in the world, owned by American and British companies, and the governments of Saudi Arabia, and Iraq. At the head of the gulf is Kuwait, another oil empire. The question is often asked, "Who is the richest man in the world, the King of Arabia or the Sheik of Kuwait?"

Although Bahrein and the area around it pours out more oil than any other region on the face of the globe, few people, Lowell Thomas says, know the name of the capital city, which is Manama. And the Bahrein ruler at that time was a Persian Gulf prince whose lineage he declared went back to the days when the caliphs ruled in Baghdad, perhaps even farther, all the way back to Adam and Eve. His name? Sheik Suleiman Hamid el Kalifah, Prince of Pearls and Oils.

Planes fly daily from the Persian Gulf to the United States. Beneath those layers of coral and sand flows liquid gold.

What happens to the wealth pocketed by these Arabs? At Bahrein much has been wisely spent by the Prince who was benign in many ways. His able British adviser had seen to it that a third of the oil money went into roads, schools, hospitals, and sanitation.

Lowell Thomas also visited King Saud at Riyadh, whose income averaged a million dollars a day. The first thing that impressed him about the Saudi capital, he said, was the number of automobiles and the modern metaled strip from the airport into the city. Most of the cars are of an expensive American make. King Saud and his father, the late King Ibn Saud, bought fleets of Cadillacs for their many wives. The present ruler and his many sons—with members of their families—have them.

The guest was greeted by one of the King's advisers, who showed Lowell Thomas the royal school building which only the sons of the King attend. Each boy had his own Cadillac, a driver, and a personal servant to go to school with him. Why a servant in school? The servant stands at hand to pour his young master a "spot of tea" whenever the boy feels the need. However, each boy has had his breakfast with his own particular mother before starting off to school.

The boys are brought up in an almost puritanical manner. Their lives of primitive simplicity, as to liquors, for instance, stem from a religious reformer, Ibn Abdul Wahab, who taught the austere life. But he was a reformer who did not include monogamy in his austerity program.

While visiting with the King and his many sons, Lowell was asked how many sons he had. He replied, of course, that he had one but wished he had twenty-seven. Prince Fahid, Saud's eldest, remarked in perfect English that he thought one was enough. Although Fahid was the crown prince, he was not destined to become king, for even then the next in line for the crown was King Saud's brother, Prince Feisal, who in recent years had taken over the reins of authority and recently succeeded to the throne.

At the walled city of Riyadh, Lowell Thomas was lodged in one of the King's palaces. Not only was he given a room thirty by thirty feet and twenty-five feet high, but he had a palatial reception room three times larger with ornate gilded chairs around the wall. In his bedroom he had twin beds and Oriental rugs.

Glittering chandeliers added to the elegance of his reception room, and no sooner was he settled than coffee was brought in by a giant Sudanese servant.

Then he was taken in tow by Al Foster, a tall, thin chap with a soft voice and quiet manner, an American from Portland, Oregon. Whatever was he doing deep in Saudi Arabia? Al explained that while he had come out to work for the Arabian-American Oil Company, and had been there for ten years, that for some time he had been on loan to the King, as a sort of wazir of finances in connection with the King's private life. That is, he kept track of all the Oriental rugs, furniture, automobiles and so on.

Lowell Thomas breakfasted alone at the end of a long table with about a hundred empty chairs. The meal was served by a tall, black Somali. The menu included goat cheese, olives, and pomegranates. When Al Foster came in, Lowell expressed his curiosity about the chairs since in Araby people usually sat on rugs and cushions. Al turned over a chair, on which he had written a symbol in Arabic, and reported that the chair had been made in Italy. He said that once a year he took an invoice of all the furnishings in the various palaces. He was eager to show Lowell Thomas the most attractive palace in Central Asia, built on a large oasis and called Bedeeiah.

Bedeeiah aroused the interest of the aged Abdul Aziz Ibn Saud. In fact, he liked his son's palace so much that he decided to move into it himself. The son had no choice but to allow his father to take over the exquisite palace, but he removed most of the finer things. The rough desert Bedouins who surrounded his father could ruin delicate furniture.

Al proudly showed Lowell Thomas the palace called Bedeeiah, pointing out the sloping ramps between the rooms and the different elevations in the garden. Although Ibn Saud was a giant of a man, in his later years he suffered from arthritis in his legs. Al reported that President Roosevelt gave Ibn Saud the spare wheel chair he had along at Yalta, but the chair wasn't big enough, so Ibn Saud had it copied in an adequate size; and then ramps were constructed to accommodate the electrically propelled chair.

Why, Lowell Thomas wanted to know, did Al prefer the walled capital of Riyadh to the City of Roses on the banks of the Willamette in the shadow of Mount Hood? Didn't he ever become homesick for Portland, Oregon, U.S.A.?

Al Foster had a ready if not a satisfying answer. It was a merry sort of life, full of fun and ease. King Saud liked to play pool or skee ball and often got Al out of bed late at night for a swift game. Al himself enjoyed pool. Then, too, Al played jazz on the piano in a way that delighted the King. He was not hard to please.

But Lowell Thomas was not entirely dependent on Al for his sightseeing. Ibn Saud himself took his guest for a tour of Riyadh, his capital far inland on the central plateau. Few had seen it.

As his Majesty stepped out of the limousine, a great shout went up with the cry, "Allah homma towel omr jala la telemalek!" Lowell inquired the meaning and Sheik Abdul Bulkair informed him it was their version of "God save the King!"

A courier overtook the party with a copy of the morning paper, published in Mecca and flown up in one of the King's planes. It was printed in Arabic, but Lowell Thomas noted in the middle of the front page pictures of President Eisenhower, the British Foreign Minister, Secretary Eden, and Secretary of State John Foster Dulles.

Passing the Riyadh date market and on through the narrow streets of the old city, they came to the famous gate where the tip of a spear was embedded in a massive door, a splash of blood above it. It was here that an historic event had taken place in 1902 when old King Ibn Saud, then an exile, had killed the governor and made himself king. Then he had quickly risen to be master of Arabia—thirty-eight years before the Americans found oil under the desert sand.

Officials showed Lowell Thomas a modern hospital, block after block of new government buildings, and more palaces belonging to the Saudi princes. There was an expensive modern hotel, a power plant, and a telephone building. At the railway station a flock of goats sought shade under a train on a siding. Further on, in the King's garden, great roses bloomed among the palm trees.

The group with Lowell Thomas talked and drank coffee until the voice of a Muezzin rang out from a nearby minaret. While the King led his own group in prayer, his guest strolled in the beautiful garden, fragrant with roses, then walked with the King into the brilliantly lighted banquet hall, the walls all a continuous mirror. There was room to serve several hundred at the U-shaped table. The King sat alone at the head with his top adviser, an elderly sheik, a few feet below on his left, perhaps twelve feet away, and Lowell Thomas reported, "with me on his right in relatively the same position." Then along the table on both sides of the hall sat his advisers, guests, and his twenty-seven sons. Today there are twenty or thirty more sons, and an unknown number of daughters. Hanging behind the King was a green flag with its Saudi insignia of a palm tree and crossed scimitars in gold. The table seemed spread for a banquet. But the King always dined like this when in Riyadh. Tall blacks served, all in white, including white turbans and white gloves, a servant behind each chair.

Soup was brought on, and the banquet began. The conversation turned to America. The King had once been on a forty-day trip to the United States and spoke of the Empire State Building and the Hoover Dam. He talked enthusiastically of Herbert Hoover who, he said, thought it possible to divert the waters of those two great Mesopotamian rivers, the Tigris and the Euphrates, and make a paradise out of great areas of the desert.

The dinner was most elaborate, with course following course. Yet no wine was served. There were several nonalcoholic drinks, including grape juice and ending with camel's milk. There was also pasteurized cow's milk from the royal dairy on a nearby oasis. One of the courses was bustard, much like wild turkey.

The dessert might have come from an American hotel. It was a large wedge of coconut cake and ice cream, topped off with dates and camel's milk. The chef turned out to be an American, from Brooklyn!

The party ended with a sprinkling of rose water on the King's hands, then on the hands of the guest, Lowell Thomas. Another servant held a brazier of glowing coals over which they could dry their hands.

The King retired to his harem.

Naturally no man was allowed to visit the harem except the king. But a few days earlier an American woman from Dharan was allowed to meet the King's wives, and said that one of them wore around her neck a diamond the size of a small ash tray. Another had a ring set with a diamond almost as large as a golf ball. All wore Parisian evening gowns, along with their bracelets, necklaces, and watches encrusted with diamonds. Living quarters were furnished in French furniture upholstered with pale pink brocade. There were rugs from Persia, and in the palace grounds were neon lights, brought from America.

While a man may have four wives, his tastes in drinking must be curbed. He is thus obeying the rules of puritanism set down by that austere leader, Ibn Abdul Wahab, back in the eighteenth century. Even in the American oil city of Dhahran the law of the Koran forbidding alcoholic beverages was strictly enforced.

While at Riyadh, Lowell Thomas made arrangements for the Cinerama crew to film the fabulous world of Arabian oil, for under the sands an ocean of petroleum had been tapped.

After the crew took their pictures, King Saud entertained all eighteen of them at luncheon in the same hall of mirrors where Lowell Thomas had been entertained. What struck the men, particularly in Saudi Arabia, were the palaces, the elaborate meals and the camel's milk.

Chapter Sixteen

Mount Everest and the Darjeeling Railroad

Mount Everest, the world's loftiest peak, could well be reckoned one of the seven natural wonders of the world. Lowell Thomas was eager to include it in his Cinerama production.

He had read much about Everest, and for a month had lived on a mountain from which he could see the world's loftiest peak. Although the Himalayan rocks are sedimentary, that is, formed by sediment deposited in water, Mount Everest is more than 29,140 feet high. It is hard to believe that this mountain was once part of the bottom of the sea.

What caused it to rise? Some titanic force surely. Scientists tell us that earthquakes are mountain builders, and the Himalayas are in an earthquake area.

The height of Everest was determined by the calculations of an Indian expert. The survey was made by Sir George Everest who was an eminent geographer engaged in Indian survey work. The peak was named after him.

Lowell Thomas making a parallel turn at Alta, Utah.

Lowell Thomas overlooking the Sahara.

Lowell Thomas and friend on dhow in Persian Gulf.

Generalissimo Chiang Kai-shek, Lowell Thomas and General Albert C. Wedemeyer

Lowell Thomas was familiar with the history of the attempts to scale the mountain. Mount Everest had seemed an unattainable goal, partly because the journey to reach the base was so difficult. It was not until the 1920's that an attempt was made to reach the summit.

Then in 1924 two explorers may have climbed the topmost pinnacle. But if they reached the top, nobody knew, for they never came back.

In spite of this tragedy, several more attempts were made, and two British planes made a first flight over in 1933. There was a climbing attempt made in 1936 and two more expeditions in 1953, all failures.

Then, almost exactly twenty-nine years after the tragedy of 1924, in June of 1953 Lowell Thomas is enabled to make this broadcast. It is significant. He could not secure Everest for his Cinerama show but he could tell of the mountain in a memorable news broadcast. Here is the story:

"All that Coronation festivity in Britain today turns out to be something unique—the like of which has never been known before. I can think of few moments in history to approach it for sheer drama. The glowing pageant of royalty, with all the splendors of centuries past—combined with an historic exploit, the achievement of one of mankind's most difficult and perilous ambitions, the conquest of Mount Everest!

"Imagine Ferdinand and Isabella celebrating some sort of magnificent jubilee when in walks a sea captain with a party of sailors—Christopher Columbus announcing the discovery of America!

"Tonight while all Britain sings 'God Save the Queen,' they are also acclaiming Hillary, the New Zealander, and Tensing, the mountain man of the high Himalayas!

"Queen Elizabeth was aroused from sleep to hear about it. She had retired on the eve of her coronation, and was to arise in a few hours for the great event. But she was gotten out of bed to be informed of the exploit which, from the beginning, had been intended as a coronation gift to her.

"The climbers had been beaten back on previous attempts but had stuck to their camp at the 27,000-foot level for one more 'go' at that ultimate summit which no human being had ever scaled before and come down to tell the tale. . . . They had to make it now or never because the monsoon was closing in, the rains which mean huge snows in the Himalayas. Moreover, they were determined to do it in time for the coronation.

"The final victory over Everest was won by a thirty-four-year-old New Zealand beekeeper, Ed Hillary—now Sir Edmund Hillary—who learned mountaineering by climbing the magnificent peaks of the south island of his own native New Zealand. He was accompanied by a fabulous native guide named Tensing, a Sherpa tribesman who, time and time again, had accompanied Everest expeditions. Tensing, the Sherpa of Nepal, had taken part in more attempts on Everest than any other man in the world.

"What a tremendous feature to accompany the pageantry of royalty in London! Far off in the Himalayas, the conquest of Everest!"

Cinerama did not get Mount Everest for its Seven Natural Wonders. Lowell Thomas had planned to have Paul Mantz fly him to the mountain, but the Indian government said no. Everest is in Nepal on the border of Tibet, and Tibet by now was dominated by the Chinese Reds. India would permit no flying whatever anywhere near the frontier of Communism, and this included most of the lofty peaks of the Himalayas.

Cinerama had to accept this fact. If absolutely necessary, Lowell Thomas could and would compromise. Nor was the crew discouraged. They were in the Himalayas, and why not do a fresh Himalaya story?

It was decided to photograph the little Darjeeling railroad. While it was not one of the seven wonders of the world, it would provide comedy relief. And, of course, the whole world had heard of Darjeeling tea. Here were the plantations that raised it.

The Darjeeling train started from a little station down on the plains. From sweltering India it climbed steep mountain slopes to its pleasant, comfortable height.

Darjeeling, as Lowell Thomas remarked, was quite a place. It had been secured by the British as part of a settlement from the potentate of Sikkim out of gratitude for being saved from the Nepalese. It became a pleasant hill station for invalided British soldiers brought up from Bengal where the weather was sweltering, and for the British Burrasahibs and memsahibs from Calcutta. When tea cultivation was started, Darjeeling became not only world famous, but prosperous as well. When it became a resort, there was need for a railroad.

British engineers performed a near miracle in building a forty-mile railroad that rose from sea level on the plains of Bengal to an altitude of 7400 feet in the Himalayas. The roadbed struggles around steep curves and slopes, winding back and forth in tight loops. It climbs to the edge of cliffs, looking down into six-thousand-foot chasms. It may look like a toy train, but it has a big name—the Himalayan-Darjeeling Railroad. It does quite a business.

On the trip up it carries rice, tea-planting supplies, hotel provisions—and tourists. Coming back it brings loads of garden vegetables, returning tourists, and, of course, tea.

Life is not always smooth or easy on the line. Disturbances include not only elephants on the tracks but sometimes tigers or even leopards.

In the twenties, Lowell Thomas had filmed the railway with a French camera. It had been a silent picture, intended to be informational. The new picture done by Cinerama needed a plot, something to carry a narrative interest—and with a degree of suspense. Humorous, if possible, decided Lowell Thomas.

At his direction, W. P. Lipscomb, the London playwright, devised a scenario. He used mountain people as characters riding the train, along with an American tourist he designated as Drowsy Dan. Drowsy Dan well deserves his encomium, for he sleeps all through the journey.

The journey begins well enough with the firemen shoveling coal into the chugging engine while out front on a small double platform stands Moe and Joe strewing sand on the tracks. The sand is necessary to secure traction on the steep slopes. Around the curves runs the train, the background fabulous Himalayan scenery.

Trouble! The train halts. There's a mama elephant asleep across the tracks, her baby beside her. Trainmen attempt to shoo her away. No result! Passengers join in the attempt. The elephants are not impressed. Then Saba, the small elephant boy, climbs up on the back of the huge pachyderm and the great beast gets up and ambles off, baby following.

The sheepish passengers start to get back into the train. But no! Alas! The train, without warning, is running backward downhill. Something has gone wrong. The brakes are not holding. It's a runaway train, speeding down the slopes, faster and faster and faster. The crowd chases after it, hoping to intercept it at some place where, due to the grade, it must slow down. But they miss. The runaway train whizzes on, a hundred miles an hour, two hundred miles an hour, three hundred miles an hour—faster than any train ever went before.

Of course, it is the trick photography that accounts for the speed. Finally, as it must, it comes to a stop.

Drowsy Dan, who has slept all through the trip, blinks and starts to leave, thinking he has arrived at his destination, Darjeeling. He can't believe that he is back where he started from.

It took ten days of work to produce this merry comedy thriller. The Cinerama crew hired a complete train for the job. The workers painted the locomotive a bright red so it would show up in the picture against the gorgeous scenery. Naturally, they had to hold up traffic and schedules, but the Indian authorities did not complain.

They wanted to develop Darjeeling as a tourist resort. And what would be better advertising than the comedy drama of their railroad? This picture would bring in tourists who would spend their vacation money in Darjeeling.

Said Lowell Thomas, "That's the story of how we got our comedy and thriller—but the clouds hid Mount Everest, which we never did get."

Chapter Seventeen

The Great Wall of China

Ever since he studied geography as a youngster in Cripple Creek, Colorado, Lowell Thomas had been interested in the Great Wall of China. This was one man-made wonder that no one could question. Even the Great Pyramid was a pygmy in comparison with this meandering Asiatic giant. A great deal of it still stood and could be photographed for Cinerama. What a colossal project the Great Wall was—and still is! The traveler may see a goodly part of it.

China, of course, lies north of Tibet, and the vast rampart of masonry extends from near Peking westward into the middle of North China. With all its windings, it is two thousand miles long. Its height, from twenty to fifty feet, and its width, fifteen feet. There are two parapets along the entire top, one for either side. Between them lies a roadway, twelve feet wide.

As planned, a man could drive the entire two thousand miles in a chariot and be shielded all the way from the missiles of enemies by the parapet. Designed to keep the intruder of the Middle Ages out, it was a stupendous production. Everything that a builder could conceive was provided. At regular intervals there were tall watchtowers on top of the walls, 24,000 towers in all.

The Great Wall follows the topography of the country up hill and down dale, even to climbing a mountain five thousand feet high.

Every engineer admits that the amount of treasure and toil it took to create the prodigy is incalculable. The men needed to maintain it ran into fantastic figures. Engineers estimate that, stationed a yard apart, it would have taken three million soldiers to protect it. Military men reason that the method of defense was to mobilize troops at a threatened point.

Scholars will remember the Emperor Shih Hwang-ti who founded the Chin Dynasty in the third century B.C. for two things: he built the Great Wall, and he burned the books, both of them foolish.

When he seized the throne, he overthrew the political system maintained by the scholars of the land. They followed the tradition of Confucius whose philosophies had flourished for several centuries. But Emperor Shih Hwang-ti had decided that Confucian literature was inimical to his regime and he ordered the destruction of the Confucian classics.

This act was known as the famous—or infamous—Burning of the Books.

To protect his people from the barbarians on the plains of Mongolia, he boasted that he built The Wall. Neither the Burning of the Books nor the building of the Great Wall served the purpose he desired, and after the Emperor's death, scholars brought back the classics. They had been hidden, to be saved and now were copied. Confucianism was restored. Only Shih Hwang-ti's reputation suffered. The scholars naturally were the historians who recorded his deeds, and surely they could not speak well of him.

As for the Great Wall, it did not keep out the barbarians. They came in from the north and conquered China again and again. The Mongols invented movable towers on which they could scale the walls.

Lowell Thomas refers to The Great Wall as a monumental futility.

Futile, too, was his attempt to catch up with General Jimmy Doolittle in China. He had planned to fly around the world with him, but he missed him in New York, Casablanca, Egypt, India, and Calcutta, only to learn, for all his efforts, that his friend, General Jimmy, had been hurriedly called back to Washington.

When they failed to meet in India, Lowell Thomas decided to take a plane over the Hump, over the Himalayas. It was at the time that the United States was helping Generalissimo Chiang Kai-shek's army round up thousands of small Central Asian horses to use for transporting supplies and equipment that could not be handled by trains or by air.

The plane in which he rode was a DC3, piloted by a veteran China National Airways flier, a Captain Pottschmidt. From Kunming he flew northward over wild regions, crossing the gorges of great rivers of

Asia, the Salween, the Mekong, the Yangtse, and the Yellow River, over scenery not unlike the Grand Canyon of the Colorado.

During the flight the plane landed in a pasture near the walled city of Sichang. A couple of Tibetans, Gunga and Donga, had brought a string of horses from Tibet and were now faced with the long trek home. The Captain offered to give them a lift. However, the plane ran into stormy weather. Forced off course for hundreds of miles, the plane landed at an airfield outside the walled city of Chamdu. Although they had experienced an airborne adventure, Gunga and Donga now had an even longer walk home.

Lowell Thomas reporting by short wave, said:

"Here I am, still on the other side of the world. Although I have tried many times to get through by short wave from Chungking, the Chinese International Broadcasting beam isn't so very international. I doubt if it covers half of China. The head of it, Mike Pung, told me we would be heard in the States. But later I learned that not a word got through. The station was not powerful enough. And in hot Chungking, at 6:45 in the morning, that's discouraging.

"Well, in the ten days or so that I've spent in China, I visited by air and by Jeep the provinces of Yunman and Sikang, and also the provinces of Szechwan, Kweichow, and Kwangsi.

"The ranking American general in the field in China is Major General Bob McClure, a stocky, ruddy-faced tough, hard-bitten veteran. He asked me to accompany him on a trip, by Jeep and by munitions carrier, to one of the wildest parts of China, the mountains of Kwangse where a lot of recent fighting had been going on.

"One object of the trip was to take General Ho Yin-chin, former minister of war and now chief of staff of the Chinese armies, down to that corridor. Also General Yu Fei-peng, minister of communications.

"General Yu Fei-peng is a Chinese notable of large dimensions. If he wore the silk coat of a mandarin of old, and if you put him in a sedan chair, he would look just like an old Chinese print.

"It was blazing hot. The road was bumpy and dusty. General Yu, in his Jeep, perspired copiously and fanned himself furiously. Every time the Jeep would pull up because of a roadblock caused by pack trains or water buffalo, General Yu's aid would run to the nearest stream or paddy field and bring back a basin of water wherewith the great man would refresh himself and get ready for the next lap with its clouds of dust and the bumps that were mighty hard on the sacroiliacs of General Yu Fei-peng and General Ho Yin-chin and your reporter and General Lacey Murrow, brother of commentator Edward R. Murrow, with whom he rode.

"At Machang we found a detachment of our American lads living in a Chinese temple, and then on to Tuyun, Tushan, and Nantan."

"A day or so later, we were in the country of the Chocolate Drop Mountains—I named them that—thousands of separate peaks like green rice croquettes on a great platter with paddy fields in between. Until recently, Europeans never came here, except an occasional missionary carried in a sedan chair.

"An American aviator recently had a miraculous escape in these mountains. He was Lieut. Col. William E. Blankenship, second in command of a P-51 fighter outfit. The Colonel had been strafing the Japs at Liuchow. In this sector even pursuit planes carry bombs. Bill, coming in low over Liuchow, spotted a camouflaged area. Releasing a bomb, he hit the bull's-eye, and up went an ammunition dump. With the tremendous explosion not only up went the dump but down came Colonel Bill and his plane. A wing was coming off, but it held till he could climb a thousand feet or so, and then he bailed out; whereupon, the air colonel came down kerplunk in the mud of a rice paddy. Half devoured by mosquitoes, it was four days before he located a friendly military outfit in those Chocolate Drop Mountains."

And there had, unfortunately, been no Cinerama camera to record the story.

Chapter Eighteen

Memories That Bless and Burn

A later Cinerama trail did lead across southern Asia from India into Indo-China and inner Cambodia, to a lost jungle empire falling into decay. Once there had been a glorious kingdom, the empire of the Khmers, who probably came from India. The earliest ruler, still a legend, was King Yacovarman of the ninth century who could vanquish a tiger or an elephant with his bare hands. He, it was claimed, was the one who built a fortress city for his capital and called it Angkor Thom. It was a regal capital indeed, with its palaces, shrines, monuments, and battlements.

But it was the warrior sovereign Jayavarman who proved to be the strong and idealistic ruler. He it was who built the Angkor Vat, a temple outside the city. It is considered a masterpiece of Khmer architecture and sculpture, one of the wonders of the world. In spite of his attainments, Jayavarman abdicated his throne to become a Buddhist monk.

But all too soon the glory of the Khmers was gone. The Siamese and the Thais revolted and in the fourteenth century Angkor Thom, the palace city, became a deserted city. As a successful enemy came in, everybody left—the court, the priests, and the rest of the people.

Angkor Vat, the great temple, was abandoned. Creepers climbed the walls as the jungle closed in. Plants sprouted in ever-widening cracks between stones. Trees grew up among the statues.

Only recently French explorers rediscovered the ruins and attempted to reclaim the once massive structures. Various religions had once taken hold in this region, but today in Cambodia the belief is in the Light of Asia. The Cinerama camera filmed a scene at the restored Angkor Vat, of yellow-robed monks doing a Buddhist ceremonial dance.

Then the Cinerama trail continued from Southwest Asia on to Hong Kong and on to Japan. Lowell Thomas went ahead of the camera crew to plan for the filming of the land of Fujiyama. His description of this near perfect mountain gives a vivid picture:

"You might guess that some cosmic sculptor had created this mountain. He knew how to pick a site, flat land on the shore of a bay with no surrounding peaks to obscure the grandeur of this solitary cone. He was also versed in geometry. The ideal shape of a mountain is a cone, and Fujiyama is almost a mathematical one with a flattened top. Every proper mountain should be snowclad, and the summit of Fuji is draped beautifully with gleaming snow. Our cosmic sculptor had a proper sense of decoration. He was Vulcan, lord of volcanoes, who built mountains by hurling forth subterranean fire and lava."

Anyone who has ever beheld Fujiyama has regarded its perfection with awe. It is not surprising that Japan thinks of it as a sacred mountain and in Japanese art, Fujiyama is the most familiar symbol.

The Cinerama crew, headed by director Walter Thompson, made Fujiyama a special goal. Like many another mountain, Fujiyama was often veiled by clouds. Day after day, following the arrival of the Cinerama crew, the fickle mountain remained swathed in mist. Luckily, the crew kept cameras ready, and it was well they did, for suddenly, one day, the winds parted the curtain of clouds and Fujiyama stood there in all her glory. Never had she seemed more beautiful.

Walter Thompson knew that he had a masterpiece of photography. He was well aware of that "curious quality of grace and quaintness" that the Japanese have, and he took a film of Japanese girls in one of those oddly beautiful gardens with their flowers and stunted trees and mossy stones. To make it all a bit more modern, he rounded up a couple of American soldiers from the U.S.A. and had them trailed by youngsters in the bright costumes of Old Japan. This picture, presented by Cinerama of the two GI's with the little tots, the background a lovely countryside in pastel colors, and Geisha girls performing a musical extravaganza, is a thing of sheer beauty. It is followed by pictures of venerable temples and Shinto shrines along with Buddhist shrines—all part of peaceful living, making it hard to vizualize the horrors of a recent war.

Yet Lowell Thomas, for all his smiling approval of the lovely scenes being enacted, must have been aware of dark memories that intruded into the brightness. Back of that wonderful peace was a story of treachery and cruelty.

It is well to look into his thoughts and evoke tragic remembrances: Here he was in 1945 reporting from the Far Eastern battlefronts:

"I am broadcasting this from the base of a famous volcano, right at the front door to Japan. The name of the volcano is Suribachi. From this you will know that I am coming through by short wave from a spot that has cost us more lives for its size than any place on earth, the island of Iwo Jima.

"The Marines came in here last February 19th. It was on the 23rd day that they took Suribachi. They raised the flag just a few yards from this mobile transmitter, the truck from which I am broadcasting. That was the day the photograph was taken with which you are all familiar (the picture published everywhere of four Marines raising the American flag on the summit). Up to March 15th some four thousand of our boys had been killed there and more than fifteen thousand were wounded or missing.

"Since then they have been digging Japs out of caves that abound on and around this mountain that juts out of the sea. They have killed three thousand in recent days, bringing the Japanese dead on Iwo Jima up to around twenty-five thousand. All dead, except less than two hundred taken prisoners!

"I flew in here yesterday with the Chief of the Army Air Forces, General 'Hap' Arnold, and the man who commands our air forces fighting the Japs in this part of the world, General Barney Giles. One of the first things General Arnold did before he climbed to the summit of the volcano was to decorate some of our airmen. After the landing, the Japs remaining in the caves still made raids, suicide raids. Jap planes didn't come over last night, by the way. But here is the way one citation reads that has to do with a surprise Jap attack:

"Upon being awakened in the early morning by the sound of heavy fire, Lieutenant Coons discovered that the enemy had begun firing and throwing grenades into the tent area (Lieutenant Coons—Joe Coons—from Minnesota, is a tall, broad-shouldered airman, with high cheekbones and deep sunken eyes). With total disregard for his own safety, Lieutenant Coons opened fire on the invaders with his pistol from inside the tent! Then the citation tells how he went on out of the tent to get a better shot. In fact, he moved from one enemy position to another, throwing hand grenades and firing his pistol. Crawling over the rough lava surface (the island is all lava), he crawled to within a few feet of an enemy entrenchment containing about twenty-six Japs. Of these he proceeded to kill more than half. For this, General Arnold awarded him a Silver Star."

From Iwo Jima Lowell Thomas went on to Okinawa, from where he gave the listening world another report:

He says, "I was on the island or watching the fighting from the air at the time the Japs were making their last stand. The Marines and doughboys were cutting them up into smaller and smaller pockets with heavy losses on both sides.

"I was there when General Simon Bolivar Buckner was killed. In fact, I had just missed the General at his headquarters that morning, or I would undoubtedly have been with him. But I was delayed, and his Chief of Staff, Brigadier General Elwyn Post, asked me to stay and talk and have lunch and await General Buckner's return.

"The G-2 in charge of psychological warfare joined us and told us that more and more of the Japs were beginning to surrender. Even their officers at last showed a distaste for suicide by throwing themselves off cliffs, walking into the sea, or making fatal banzai charges. Although some were still dying blindly, organized resistance had been broken.

"About the death of General Buckner: his 'number evidently was up.' For the Japs had only one gun, one mortar, still in action. With it they lobbed over one shell, and that got the General . . ."

Lowell Thomas seldom philosophizes over his own reports but in this case he gives his personal reactions:

He said, "What I saw and heard in those days at places like Iwo Jima and Okinawa gave me an evil feeling of how masses of human beings can hate each other with a rage for collective murder. Normally, American soldiers in war are about as decent as possible in organized killing. But the Jap atrocities, their fiendish treatment of helpless prisoners, forced our people in the Pacific battles to be almost as merciless as the Japs themselves."

And now began the atomic era, which Lowell Thomas saw as inevitable. The blast at Hiroshima, followed by a second bomb at Nagasaki, was to result in the Japanese surrender.

Only one atomic bomb, a four hundred pound one, was let loose at Hiroshima, but it destroyed four square miles of the city and caused a hundred thousand casualties. The Japanese report was as vivid as a Lowell Thomas description: "The impact of the bomb was so terrific that practically all living things, human and animal, were literally seared to death by the tremendous heat and pressure engendered by the blast."

Lowell Thomas pointed out how the Oriental mind was so clearly understood by General MacArthur. The people, with due regard to the victor, accepted the enemy commander as a benign autocrat. His imposing presence, Lowell Thomas indicated, was a big factor in his acceptance.

To watch the two GI's with the brightly clad Japanese children as shown on Cinerama could almost make one forget the whole frightful war in the Pacific.

The Cinerama crew in Kamakura delighted in the giant statue of the sitting Buddha with the peaceful smile. The statue, they saw, was of bronze, forty feet in height and weighing, they learned, more than a hundred tons. Not only in Kamakura but in many places around the countryside, the crew saw countless Buddhas. Who was Buddha? The history, they found, was most interesting.

Buddha and Buddhism date back, they learned, to the sixth century, A.D. Prince Gautama, scion of a royal house, had become disillusioned with earthly pleasures. He, the Enlightened One, taught a doctrine of involved metaphysics. It involved reincarnation, then escape from self into nothingness. Simplicity was all important, the exact opposite of the elaborate system of the Brahmins. Its most significant creed was the rejection of caste and the acceptance of all men as equal and on equal terms. Strangely enough, although it rejected all images, there soon were many statues of Buddha. The sole symbol had always been the lotus flower in all its purity, but people must have needed a more earthy symbol. Greek sculptors formed the first images. The serene expression was Greek. The features and cross-legged posture were Oriental. The attitude was one of meditation. It is to be noted that the formal, draped folds of the Buddhist garment are classic Greek.

Flying halfway 'round the world from the serenity of Buddha in country villages to the carnival gaiety of Rio made for a spectacular change. Lowell Thomas' Cinerama crew was enchanted, especially so as they were lucky enough to find Rio in high carnival spirits. The streets were full of wild dancing to the rhythm of the Brazilian samba.

Lowell Thomas was thrilled with the fantastically beautiful air shots—the magnificent ocean beach with Sugar Loaf in the background, and, most spectacular of all, the great statue of Christ the Saviour on top of Corcovado, the famous mountain. The Saviour looked down on the city, arms outstretched as if in blessing.

Paul Mantz made an unexpected report for Cinerama as he flew to Rio. Along the coast of Brazil, they suddenly discovered a battle going on between the sand and the jungle. The yellow sand advances like an army into the jungle, and it looks very much, on these unusual pictures, as if the sand is winning against the jungle.

Even more spectacular were Cinerama shots of Iguazu Falls where the borders of Argentina, Brazil and Paraguay meet. The wide Iguazu River comes to a line of cliffs and tumbles over, not in one mighty surge, but in a broad front of giant cascades. Each cascade is like a mighty falls in itself, a splendid outpouring shot with rainbows. Cinerama shows its size and its splendor, twice as wide as Niagara and half again as high.

Surely, as Paul Mantz flew down the gorge to make the delightful picture of sheer beauty in movement and color, he must have felt that he was recording one of the Seven Wonders of the Modern World.

Its beauty, our traveler thinks, is best expressed by a Spanish lawyer, Humberto Maliza, who says, "Looking at Iguazu—moved by such beauty, such grandeur . . . we wish we had been born poets so as to sing with inspired verse the imposing sound of the waters . . . the pearl of its lymphs, forming the rainbow upon being struck by the golden rays of the sun . . . the spotless whiteness and purity of the currents, pure as the conscience of good men, and so render homage to their Supreme Creator, One who more properly ought to be called the Great Architect of the Universe."

Angel Falls in Venezuela was on the agenda for Cinerama. The crew knew that South America had the highest waterfalls in the world, but Angel Falls had more than height. It had the sort of mystic jungle beauty that poets dream of. Lowell Thomas himself waxed poetic.

"The Cinerama air shots of Angel Falls are a phantasmagoria—a classic version of the 'Lost World.' Deep in the jungle and mountain wilderness of southeastern Venezuela is an immense plateau with lofty cliffs for walls, like several of our own Western mesas put together, on top of each other. Down the sides of the 'Lost World' a number of waterfalls topple, the loftiest a stream that plunges 3212 feet, twenty times as high as Niagara."

Strange as it may seem, Angel Falls was discovered by an American. In 1937, Jimmy Angel, a bush pilot, was flying his plane in the Caribbean area. His services were for hire. While seeking gold, he found Angel Falls by accident.

His story, as related by Lowell Thomas, is an exciting and intriguing one, and the ending has the listener wondering. It happened that in Panama City there was an old, weatherbeaten prospector by the name of Bob Williamson. He told of a place loaded with gold nuggets in the mountains of Venezuela. He had discovered the area in his wanderings and wanted to return for more gold to replenish his supply. It was just a matter of getting in and picking up the nuggets, he said. He engaged Jimmy Angel to fly him in for $5,000. Jimmy said he would fly anywhere for $5,000.

The trip took the two of them into uncharted country. The old prospector pointed out the route, and sure enough, he picked up pocketfuls of lumps of glittering yellow. Then they flew out.

Were the lumps of glittering yellow real gold? You bet they were! Bob Williamson cashed them in for $27,000, then died two months later, leaving his money behind but taking his secret with him. What was the exact location of the fabulous nugget field?

In New York City later on, Jimmy Angel looked up Lowell Thomas and told him what seemed like a tall tale. BUT his story was verified when the "Lost World" and the highest waterfall were located.

Thomas Gilliard of the American Museum of Natural History led an expedition that explored the plateau and measured the height of Angel Falls—named after Jimmy Angel, the discoverer.

Lowell Thomas said he'd never forget that wild tale that Jimmy Angel told him in New York City. Now, twenty-five years later, in 1955, Cinerama was making a picture of Angel Falls.

What of the gold? The treasure-trove of nuggets is yet to be found. BUT IT'S THERE—SOMEWHERE.

Chapter Nineteen

Into Tibet's Forbidden City

Lowell Thomas and his son were among the last Westerners to see Tibet before its brutal occupation by Mao Tse-tung's Red Chinese army that shelled, not only the magnificent Potala, the Dalai Lama's winter palace, but wrecked the three largest monasteries in the world, Drepung, Sera, and Ganden. It was to their credit and even more to their satisfaction, that the two Lowells made it their special mission to alert the world to the impending danger; for Red China had its greedy eye on the gentle, kindly Tibetans, their vast lofty country, their border with India, and their century-old treasures. Lhasa had been the capital of the Hermit Theocracy, and an almost forbidden city. Their leaders feared the Red Chinese, and with reason. Help and understanding might come from one far-off source, from Americans, if they knew the danger. Lowell Thomas and his son were invited to visit "forbidden" Lhasa, to be made welcome, and maybe bring help, later.

The great adventure began in August of 1949. Lowell Thomas and his son gathered a train of mules and bearers at Gangtok in Sikkim on the southern slopes of the Himalayas. To cover the rough mountain trails they had to depend on the Tibetan mule, the yak, and the rugged small horses of central Asia.

Ahead rose the most formidable mountain barrier in the world. The start was pleasant, bells jangling, muleteers cracking their whips as they shouted commands. There was an air of freshness and eagerness in the atmosphere. The ponies jolted along the roads that led ever upward.

The horses that the two L. T.'s rode were soon picking their way carefully along trails that soon narrowed and clung to dizzy canyon walls. Had they slipped and lost their footing, they would have plunged into rocky gorges thousands of feet below.

Sometimes the trails were so steep and narrow that everyone in the party had to walk single-file, hugging the cliffs. There were landslides to be passed over, streams to be forded, and at Natu La, the first pass, 15,000 feet high, they found breathing a bit difficult in the rarefied air.

"Where's the border?" Lowell Junior inquired.

The caravan leader pointed to a yak-hair rope on which fluttered brightly colored prayer flags. These symbols of Buddhist piety were the only guardians of the Tibetan frontier, the only "wall" to keep out the invader.

"We rode under the prayer flags," Lowell Thomas

later reported, "and as simply as that we entered Tibet."

The muleteers began to raise the sacred chant, "Om Mani Padme Hum," which the Thomases were to hear over and over in the land of the Lamas. The words translated, they learned, were "Hail to the Jewel in the Lotus" and they were sung or chanted for the purpose of uniting the soul of the believer with his divinity.

Once over this pass they went downward into a great deep valley and from then on they were in Tibet.

As the days passed, and they again climbed up and up to the Tibetan plateau, they reveled in the joy of being in a land that not many Westerners had ever seen. The Tibetan hospitality never failed, for word of their coming had been sent from Lhasa, and the caravan was greeted with gifts of food and ceremonial scarves in every town and at every monastery. People stared and smiled along the trail, and stuck out their tongues, in the traditional Tibetan greeting.

Each night they spent in a Tibetan home. This usually was two stories high, the family living on the upper floor, the animals housed below—chickens, goats, cows, yaks and huge snarling dogs, the fierce Tibetan mastif. There were no chimneys to carry off the smoke from the clay stove and no other heating. It was always cold at night and hot by day. The guests drank chang, Tibetan barley beer, and the hot tea in which their hosts put chunks of rancid yak butter.

The Tibetan farmers were proud of their yaks, and no wonder. For centuries the yak has been Tibet's trade-mark. This shaggy-haired, bison-like animal for centuries has drawn the primitive Tibetan plows, furnished milk for the children, butter for the hot tea, yak hair for clothing, for carpets and tents, yak skin for leather, and even for boots. Here is a tireless, surefooted animal that can carry heavy loads over the dizzy Himalayan passes and the great Tibetan plateau.

Their trail first dropped into the lush Chumbi Valley. After the rugged mountain passes and the cold winds that swept over Natu La, it was a surprise to see flowery pastures and animals in the underbrush—weasels and rabbits. The flowers were a riot of color and fragrance. Oddly enough, there was a daisy of such heavy aroma that it gave one a headache if sniffed too enthusiastically. In the trees, birds sang and white-faced monkeys chattered.

The caravan pressed on to Yatung where the Sikkimese turned back. With another group of mules, muleteers, and a few yaks, the travelers continued their journey, climbing up to Phari, then on to the city of Gyantse, over more passes, through more rivers, and at last a final night on the trail spent near the world's largest monastery, Drepung, meaning "The Rice Heap," with its 10,000 monks.

A few miles farther, rounding a bend—there, before them, rose the golden-domed Potala, and spread out around it, the Forbidden City. They were nearing Lhasa! A city straight out of the Middle Ages!

Never again, in all their travels, would they be likely to see a sight so incredible and unreal. It was hard to withdraw their gaze from the gleaming Potala.

Entering the gate, they journeyed along the streets of a city that endless travelers have tried and failed to reach.

No longer were they visiting a people living in yak hair tents and crude huts. Here was a city of three and four-story houses with flat roofs and whitewashed walls decorated with prayer flags. Within they found them furnished with chairs and tables, and other things from India, and from Persia, and from China. Even the poorest dwelling had its treasures, its prayer wheels and its sacred figurine of the Lamaist religion. The people of Tibet were deeply and honestly devoted to their form of Buddhism.

"Not a wheel in Lhasa!" Lowell Junior observed. "Not a single automobile! Not a horse-drawn buggy! Not even a pushcart—but, they are not backward; they simply prefer the time-honored traditions of their ancestors. And then—roads could bring invaders."

The market place or bazaar drew crowds that bought everything from tea to silks and ornaments.

The two guests from the other side of the world were escorted to a villa on the banks of the Kyu Chu River, and showered with gifts.

Their first fleeting glimpse of the Dalai Lama was at Norbu Linga, the god-king's summer palace. It was the time of the annual festival and the two Americans became part of the throng of Tibetan visitors who came to watch an ancient and classic drama. The actors wore brilliant costumes and ferocious masks. The onlookers sat on the ground and ate barley bread, yak cheese and rice. Everybody drank buttered tea.

The Dalai Lama was only sixteen at the time, but he was adored by courtiers and common people alike. The visitors from America were told they would be granted an audience.

But first they were allowed to visit the medical college on Iron Hill. Here Tibetan physicians studied to learn the incantations that were supposed to cure the sick. But they also became versed in herbs and their uses, herbs with authentic medicinal properties.

Most impressive was the Potala, a palace so unusual that no building in the world could quite compare with it. This winter palace of the Dalai Lama rose from the valley to the top of a lofty peak, looking as though it were a part of the hill. It reached nine hundred feet into the blue sky, two thirds the height of the Empire State Building, with no iron or steel to hold it up.

The lower walls were whitewashed, relieved by bright crimson of upper stories outside the holy chapels. At the summit, golden domes gleamed in the sunlight; under these domes are the tombs of previous Dalai Lamas.

They were told there are a thousand rooms in the palace. The two travelers from a far country walked up and down dozens of stairways and through countless corridors, all the while hearing the monotonous chanting of monks and the eerie clash of gongs and cymbals.

From the roof they looked down on Lhasa with its narrow, winding streets, and at its river, the Kyu Chu, one of the larger tributaries of the Tsang-po which runs east across Tibet for a thousand miles before plunging south through the Himalayas to the plain of Hindustan, where it becomes the Brahmaputra and flows on to the Bay of Bengal.

The visit to the Dalai Lama, or the Living Buddha, was the most important event to which the visitors looked forward. Here is the radio account as sent across the Himalayas by Lowell Thomas, Sr.:

"Two hours before the time for the audience, our escort arrived. It was headed by two nobles of the court, Rimshi Kypup and Dorje Changwahba. In their bright red and gold gowns and hats, and with turquoise in their ears and hair, they were most impressive.

"Off went the cavalcade with all of us mounted on gaily caparisoned horses and mules. Ahead pranced two outriders in wide, scarlet hats, to clear the way. Next rode our two nobles, to whom all the common people bowed as we passed. Then came the two of us, strange beings at whom everyone stared.

"Behind us rode four of our entourage who had made the journey with us from Sikkim on the other side of the Himalayas. They were carrying for us the presents we had brought. These included two tiger skulls, teeth, snarl and all, set in silver and gold. These we had bought in Siam from a Bangkok silversmith, one for the Dalai Lama and another, a little smaller, for the regent. We also had a folding traveling alarm clock, and a new-type raincoat from America for the Dalai Lama! In addition to these we had a bag of coins, in a white scarf, a symbolic gift you must always take.

"It would be an unthinkable breach of etiquette not to bring presents. Then when we leave Tibet, we understand the Dalai Lama and the regent will send presents to us.

"Arriving at the palace gate, dismounting before the stone dragons, we entered with a stream of monks and nobles, all in robes and hats of red and gold. From the entrance we proceeded along an avenue of flowers to an outer court where we sat for an hour, drinking tea and watching the arrival of the lamas, the priests, the cabinet ministers, and other nobles as they filed into the audience chamber where they must appear every morning to greet his Holiness, although they never utter a word, merely drink yak butter tea, bow low many times, and chant.

"Monks on the roof blew weird tenor notes on trumpets of brass, then deeper notes on conch shells until they worked up to the deep rumble that came from brass horns, eight or ten feet long—so long and heavy, in fact, that they were supported on a golden stand. These gave forth deep, thundering blasts such as one might expect to hear announcing the end of the world.

"A line of a dozen or so monks formed at the entrance. We were told to fall in behind them, also our servants with the presents. After us, fifty or more Tibetans, eager to receive the blessings of their ruler whom they regard as the incarnation of Chenrezi, the Buddha of Mercy!

"Inside, through a haze of incense, we could see the Dalai Lama on his throne. He smiled, and to our surprise, kept smiling at us all during the ceremony.

"In a moment I was standing directly under him, holding a white scarf across my hands. In less time than it takes to tell about it, the lord chamberlain placed certain symbols on the scarf. These, the Dalai Lama took, one after the other. The first, shaped like three cones or mountains, we later learned, was to represent the world. The others were placed on my scarf and then whisked off. One was an image to represent the body, another, a book, to represent the mind. Then the Dalai Lama took my silk scarf, after which he touched his hands to my head, giving me his blessing! The same was done for Lowell, Jr., who followed me. Next we went through the same ritual with the regent who sat on a lower throne nearby.

"And all through the ceremony the great horns thundered from the roof.

"From cushions on the floor, near the throne, we watched the others in the line, shuffling along, none daring to look up. Instead of touching these with his hands, the Dalai Lama flicked them with a tassel on the end of a rod. He touches only monks and distinguished visitors. All common folk and all women—even including wives of nobles and cabinet ministers—get the tassel treatment. One nun is the only exception, the Diamond Sow, or the Thunderbolt, who presides over an all-male monastery. She is the only female regarded as the incarnation of Buddha. Her monastery is at Yamdrok Tso, the Turquoise Lake.

"As the Dalai Lama flicked the tassel, he smiled repeatedly at us. Only a few Europeans and Americans have been granted an audience with a Dalai Lama. Since he is only a sixteen-year-old boy, I suppose he was as curious about us as we were about him.

Lowell Thomas, Jr. and Lowell Thomas with Tibetan nobles and monk cabinet member, in front of the Potala in Lhasa, Tibet in 1959.

Lowell Thomas with friend in New Guinea.

The Dalai Lama and Lowell Thomas

Lowell Thomas and Tibetan actors.

"One of the most colorful moments came after the shuffling line of Tibetans had been hustled from the room. Monks brought us bowls of rice. We flicked a few grains to the right. Then one taste. That was all, merely ceremonial.

"Next our official host, Dorje, sat cross-legged like Buddha before the throne. Into his own wooden bowl, which he brought from under his robe, a monk poured yak-butter tea. Dorje downed it with one gulp and then prostrated himself three times before the Dalai Lama, bumping his head on the floor. Only after this was over did the Dalai Lama drink some of the tea. Dorje, we learned later, was acting for us. His was the responsibility of proving to his lord and sovereign that the tea contained no poison. In the past there have been Dalai Lamas who have been poisoned.

"The lord chamberlain placed red scarves around our necks—which we were told was a special distinction. One of his Holiness' seven-foot bodyguards roared out a command, and the formal audience was at an end.

"We then spent an hour with the Dalai Lama in the palace gardens, taking motion pictures of the number one Living Buddha, the fourteenth Dalai Lama, who comes from Kumbum, near Lake Koko Nor, along the undefined Tibet-China border. His full name is Getson Nwgang Lobsang Tengin Gyspso Dhepal Sangpo."

The stay in Lhasa was all too short for the two Americans who had been made welcome in the forbidden city. Lowell Thomas, Sr. had to get back to his radio job in New York. Leave of absence from sponsors was limited.

Father and son made ready to leave. Surely they had no premonition of disaster.

Fourteen years later the elder of the two again visited the Dalai Lama, this time at Dharamsala in northwestern India, where he now lives in exile. He found him a mature and wise man who devotes all his time to the welfare of other Tibetans who have been lucky enough to escape from the Red tyranny.

Chapter Twenty

Return from Tibet

Although dedicated to radio, television finally made its demands on Lowell Thomas. Through this medium he presented his series of "High Adventure," many of them breathtaking for excitement and interest. But none compared with the trip into the forbidden country of Tibet during which he and his son were received as honored guests by the Dalai Lama.

Former adventures stood out for drama. There was the visit among the cannibals of New Guinea. As Lowell Thomas said, "They were real cannibals." At the time he was there, they had just eaten thirty-five members of a rival tribe and were replete with food and revenge. The expedition to the North Pole followed, and then odd, out-of-the-way places like Timbuktu, the Australian desert and the Mountains of the Moon. There were odd peoples, too, like the pygmies and the aborigines. Alaska was one of the favorite subjects.

Somebody asked after one of the Alaskan treks, "What's Thomas like on an expedition?" and received the answer, "He's never hurried, never speaks harshly.

He's just one of the boys. In Alaska he would go down with the crew and help bring up the equipment and supplies."

But no expedition to far-flung places and no experience with people of strange customs could compare with the trip to Tibet among the gentle people.

And now they were returning, father and son, planning the homeward trek to Hammersley Hill. And Frances Thomas' smile would warm their hearts. The hospitality had been so genuine in Tibet that it was hard to say good-by to the friends they had made in Lhasa.

The start had been well planned. They got into the primitive yak-skin boats, or coracles, that had been provided and drifted down the Kyu Chu River to Chosul. There they met the caravan that was to take them across the Tibetan plateau and the high passes through the Himalayas to Sikkim and on to Bengal. They planned to return the same way they had come, and they felt certain they could make better time. Lowell, Sr. had to be back on his radio job.

Five days later, while on the trail, tragedy struck. A horse whirled and flung Lowell Thomas, Sr. onto some rocks.

From a remote outpost Lowell, Jr. relayed the sad news:

"It happened a week ago this evening—just after crossing Karo Pass on the return from Lhasa to Calcutta. We were five days out of the holy city and two days from Gyantse, making much faster time than on the way in, thanks to a swift ride down the swollen Kyu Chu in skin coracles, a ride that carried us bobbing southward the forty miles to Chushul in six hours instead of the two and a half days it had taken us by trail. My dad and I had every hope of continuing the rapid pace and of landing in New York before the first of October.

"I remember we had just been discussing how soon we might be home—then it was that luck left us in the lurch. In Tibet it is customary to dismount and walk downhill, for they have a saying that 'he's no horse if he doesn't carry you to the top of the hill, and you're no man if you don't get off and walk going down.' So it was that we had just finished the long hike, leading our animals down to the Ralung plain from that 16,600-foot pass.

"I was in the lead when my dad, a few yards behind, decided to remount his steed. Suddenly there was a commotion and a scuffle, and I turned in time to see Pop sailing through the air to land on a pile of rocks. He had had one foot in the stirrup, the other halfway over the saddle, when the horse whirled and bolted, throwing him violently to the ground. It was the first time any such thing had happened on our long journey to the Tibetan capital.

"My dad was unable to get up, white as the snows above us, and struggling to keep consciousness. Such a mishap at an altitude above that of Europe's tallest peak—where there's a lean mixture of oxygen—can spell the end quickly. A weaker heart might not have stood the shock. He had landed on his hip on some sharp stones.

"This turn of fate caught us pretty much off guard. We had no doctor, and our first-aid kit was some miles behind in our slow-moving caravan. It was getting late—only another hour till dark and Ralung, the nearest habitation and our immediate destination, lay more than four miles across the plain. What to do? The nearest medical help was in Gyantse more than two stages away, and even that was doubtful. We could do nothing but wait there on the trail, hoping that our caravan would arrive before darkness.

"Fortunately we didn't have to wait long for the sirdar and his mules and yaks. Unloading our bedding, we got Dad wrapped up in a sleeping bag and onto an army cot. But large as our first-aid kit was, there wasn't anything to relieve his agony, nothing to ease the effects of shock—no morphine.

"Four hours later, after a painful ride through the darkness and the cold that goes with nights at these altitudes, riding that flimsy cot carried by six coolies, my father at last reached shelter. Only with the utmost difficulty and with pain to him was I able to get that cot up the rickety ladder that led to the sleeping quarters of the peasant home we were to stay in.

"That first night was one of the worst Dad had ever known—the effect of shock and exposure took the form of a high fever, accompanied by faintness; his injured hip, which we thought must be broken, gave him the very devil; no position was comfortable for him—sleep was almost impossible. It was a long, gasping night of agony and worry in just about the most out-of-the-way spot you can find—in a land whose people don't believe in doctors, who rely solely on the lamas to cure their ills through prayer.

"Next morning when Tsewong, our interpreter, and I hiked to the Ralung telephone office—and, incidentally, the presence of a phone was a lucky thing, for only a few villages along the main route from Sikkim to Lhasa are connected with a single strand of wire—I prayed that the line was not down, as it frequently is for days at a time, and that I could contact the Indian army doctor in Gyantse, based at the Mahratta garrison, and further, that I could persuade him to come to the rescue. We certainly were treading on thin ice. It was almost a matter of life and death. Without a doctor to do something to Dad's leg I could see no way to ever get him home.

"The lineman managed to rouse Gyantse, after much shouting and blowing into the ancient battery-driven outfit. Though Gyantse was only thirty-three miles away, the connection was so poor that everything had to be repeated three or four times before being understood. Yes, Dr. Bir Chrandra Pal was there, but still in bed; then someone went off to wake him up. A half hour later the doctor's voice was on the other end, and I tried frantically to make him understand who I was and what had happened, but no luck. Only Tsewong talking to his brother, a clerk at the Indian Trade Agency in Gyantse, was able to get the message through. The doctor's reply was that he'd try to come if permission for him to leave could be arranged with the Tibetan trade agent. . . . Dr. Chrandra Pal, like all his Indian colleagues, was allowed to go only seven miles beyond Gyantse—the terminus of the Indian mail courier system. So, special permission had to come from the Tibetan government if he was to come to our assistance.

"Happily, the Tibetan trade agent gave the nod and the good doctor that same day made a forced march of thirty-three miles to Ralung. Never had anyone been more welcome than Dr. Pal when he entered our cold stone hut that night at nine. Besides the usual black medical case, he brought something even more valuable to both of us—mental relief! Without an X-ray machine (and there's no such thing anywhere in Tibet) he could not tell for sure whether Dad's hip was fractured, but he said he felt certain that the injury was only muscular—torn muscles and a severe sprain—which at that time was most reassuring.

"Three more days of agony on a stretcher, jouncing over a narrow rock trail that at times was so dangerous it took ten coolies, at a snail's pace, to keep Dad from plunging down into the river far below; hour after hour, strapped to the improvised stretcher. When the sun was out he nearly roasted; when it ducked behind clouds and a cold wind brought rain, he nearly froze.

The first night out at Gobski, we had to borrow Tibetan tents, sleeping out in the cold, for a detachment of soldiers had arrived just ahead of us, had taken over all available space in the village—and in Tibet no one dares raise a finger to the soldiers, who are accustomed to making up their usual deficit in salary by helping themselves to anything. . . . The next night was better. We put up at the country home of a man who could have been a king but preferred life as a Tibetan country gentleman. "Jigme Tering, one of our hosts in Lhasa, of royal Sikkimese blood, was to have been the next Maharajah of Sikkim, but he passed it up.

At a party our last night in the Forbidden City, Jigme had invited us to spend a night on his estate seven miles out from Gyantse. . . . How much better his beds were than the narrow cots of the previous night in that cold yak-haired tent, I cannot describe! The following morning brought us to the Indian garrison in Gyantse. There Dad spent ten days in bed under the watchful eyes of Dr. Pal.

"There is probably no more primitive or remote military outpost of a modern nation than the tiny Indian station behind the tallest mountains in the world, in the forbidden kingdom of Tibet. But even so, it seemed like the comforts of paradise after those first grim days of stretcher, tent, and cots.

"And so, there's the explanation why that familiar voice won't be with you, except on recordings, for a few more weeks. The doctor thinks Dad's leg will let him take to the saddle again in a fortnight. Then he'll soon be at third base—Calcutta, where a Pan-American clipper will help him make the steal home."

In Calcutta, X rays revealed the thigh bones smashed, eight fractures at the junction with the hip. Lowell Thomas had been so stoical that nobody realized the extent of his injuries until the pictures were taken. Even so, he did not have the fractures set until he had flown back to New York with his son.

In the late fall of 1962 and the early part of 1963,

Lowell Thomas was to have another taste of Tibet and he was to see the Dalai Lama again but under sadly changed conditions. Another around-the-world journey in late fall included Australia, New Zealand, an Antarctic-South Pole expedition, then on to Indonesia, India, the Himalayas, Persia, Europe, and back to the mid-Pacific for the holidays. Lowell Thomas, Jr. and his family flew down from Alaska to join Mrs. Thomas in flowery Hawaii where the entire family spent Christmas.

One major event on that long journey was his meeting with the Dalai Lama after thirteen years. That rare visit touched off remembrance of the visit to Lhasa when the two Thomases received his blessing from an impressive throne in the gold-roofed Potala. Lowell, Sr. now found him a grown young man living in exile in northwestern India, near the borders of both Kashmir and Tibet on the Indian side of the Himalayas, at Dharamsala. He had a crew cut, wore horn-rimmed glasses, and stood six feet with a slight stoop, due to ceaseless devotions. Instead of a formal greeting, he offered both hands and began at once to express his gratitude for all the Americans had done to help his people.

Did he think that Tibet would ever again be restored to her former glory? He did—but he added, "In time."

On a second visit to the Dalai Lama in his exile, Lowell Thomas noted the dark-red upholstered chairs and divans and the artistic Tibetan tapestries on the walls of the simple dwelling, all in sharp contrast to the Potola with its thousand rooms, its golden domes and its jewels.

This time he was invited to step into what proved to be a place for prayer and meditation, a small room, but impressive. The floor was covered with rich red hand-woven Tibetan carpeting, and around the walls were sacred pictures on silk depicting the life of Buddha. At the far end of the room stood a sort of altar with an impressive golden statue of Buddha.

At the time of farewell the Dalai Lama confided one of his greatest sorrows to Lowell Thomas, the loss of the vast Tibetan library that contained countless manuscripts, laboriously written by hand in the difficult Tibetan script so like Sanskrit and often illustrated by priceless religious paintings. The library housed the age-old literature of Tibet and was more precious than all the gold and jewels the Chinese Communists had confiscated. This is one lost treasure over which the world of scholars will weep.

And it is one more proof that Communism is a destructive force, lacking in judgment and sensitivity, with no regard for the rare treasures that men preserve for the generations to come. . . . Strangely, the roads that the Tibetans feared to build were the first things the Chinese Reds constructed so they might move in their tanks and armored cars.

The Tibetans, Lowell Thomas tells us, are a happy people, and already the refugees are singing as they build roads for the Indian government. Such a people deserve to survive. But the Chinese seem determined to wipe out this unique and cultured people.

Chapter Twenty-one

A Challenge Too Great to Miss... The South Pole and the Mount Hagen Area

In October of 1962 when the Berkshire Hills were a gorgeous tapestry of gold and crimson against the blue sky, someone, inadvertently perhaps, mentioned to Lowell Thomas that he had seen just about every place on this green earth. As he sat before his microphone in his studio on Quaker Hill waiting for the signal for his newscast, he had in his bright blue eyes a peculiar gleam. He had just time to say, before going on the air, "I haven't been to the South Pole," but it was plain that a fuse had been lighted.

Within two weeks he was on his way to the land of the kiwi, as the people of New Zealand are called. The kiwi is a bird that does not fly, but Lowell Thomas was to find an intrepid flyer on hand to show him the sights. Not wanting his guest to miss any of the splendors of his native country, the pilot flew him over the rich farmlands of the Canterbury Plains where the world's finest wool is produced. There are forty million sheep in this area, all broad-backed and wearing thick wool coats.

The pilot pointed out the fiords on the west coast, and several lakes, including Lake Whakatipu, unusual because its surface is a thousand feet above the sea level, and the bottom of it several hundred feet below sea level. Like most New Zealand lakes, it is intense azure blue in color.

Even more beautiful in its setting of precipitous mountains appeared Lake Manapouri ("Waters of the sorrowing heart," the Maoris call it), a lake of some sixty square miles.

The pilot set down the plane on a gravel strip in a deep valley, and Lowell Thomas looked up at Mount Cook, New Zealand's loftiest peak, twelve thousand, three hundred and forty-nine feet. Surrounded by more than a hundred peaks, rising from sea level, the effect proved spectacular. Here, in these snow-capped mountains with great glaciers flowing down the valleys, young Edmund Hillary got his training for Everest.

Tasman Glacier, one of the longest glaciers in the world, was the Lowell Thomas goal on this trip. The glacier named for Tasman, a Dutch explorer, the first European to see these islands.

John Evans, a veteran Kiwi pilot, landed Lowell Thomas and Don Miller, a U. S. Navy Commander, near the head of Tasman Glacier, high up on Mt. Cook, warning them to beware of the jagged, sharp rocks and the crevasses. The glacier, they were told, had a plastic flow of more than a foot a day, the ice, a thousand feet deep, moving forever to the sea.

It seemed strange, in this treeless region, to find

wildlife, birds and animals. The visitors saw the mountain parrot, the kea, and hoped for a glimpse of a kiwi, a bird that seldom appears in the daytime. The kiwi, about the size of the pheasant, dates back to prehistoric times and is notable for the large egg it lays. Once ornithologists thought it extinct.

The wild animals in this part of New Zealand were nearly all imported, but, like pioneers, they quickly adapted themselves to the new environment and now overrun the valleys. These include tens of thousands of deer, also the wapiti that looks like our elk, mountain goats with black horns, and chamois, brought from the high Alps in Europe. Even the rare chamois is now so numerous that no hunting licenses are needed at any season.

Flying back to Christchurch a few days later, outside his hotel window Lowell Thomas saw that famous statue of the British explorer, Captain Robert Scott, who made the hazardous trek to the South Pole, only to perish on the return journey. What now lay ahead Lowell Thomas could only surmise. The people of Christchurch kept saying, "Oh, so you're going down to the ice!" The ice was their casual name for the Antarctic. Two admirals were to fly down, Admiral David Tyree, about to retire after three years of service, and Admiral James Reedy, about to take over, with a ceremony right at the Pole.

In a huge "Hercules" plane they flew through the night over that stormy Antarctic sea, on and on for two thousand, two hundred miles from the Operation Deep Freeze on the South island of New Zealand, all the way to the edge of the Ross ice shelf, an icy landing strip on an island off the Antarctic coast. Lowell Thomas felt himself fortunate to be traveling in a new type three-million-dollar C-130 over what the Antarctic airmen call "The Penguin Airline." The plane used on this bottom of the world run cruises at from twenty-five thousand to forty thousand feet to get above the weather, and is the first plane of great size equipped to take off or land on either wheels or skis.

The runway at McMurdo, he reports, is actually on a nearby glacier that comes down from "the coldest looking mountain you ever saw—Erebus," a mountain thirteen thousand feet high, with a smoking crater on top. Erebus has not erupted since 1880, and, although it looks close at hand in the cold, clear Antarctic air, it is actually fifty miles away.

Naturally the new arrival inquired about Little America where Admiral Byrd made his headquarters. It was still there, he learned, several hundred miles up the coast. But ice and snow had crushed the buildings, and, as the men said, the only inhabitants were ghosts. Later word came that it was on a part of the ice shelf that broke off and drifted out to sea.

McMurdo had been selected by Admiral Dufek as a more satisfactory airfield for Deep Freeze No. 1.

In announcing his arrival, his guest said, "At last I am in the Antarctic, my first visit to this, the highest, windiest, and coldest of all continents."

Admiral Tyree briefed the newly arrived group about the permanent stations the United States then had in Antarctica:

Hallet, where our people work along with a group of New Zealanders.

McMurdo on the Ross Sea, the main base and administrative center.

Byrd Station, eight hundred miles from McMurdo.

What Lowell Thomas had most wanted to see was the village under the ice at the South Pole.

He was particularly interested, too, in the proposed fifth base on the edge of Marie Byrdland, closer to the southern tip of South America, only a few hundred miles from the range of mountains named for Lowell Thomas years ago. Some day, he still has hopes of visiting those mountains—maybe this year!

Admiral Tyree's report gave the population of the Antarctic as 1163 Americans, a hundred or so from New Zealand, Australia, and England, with a French base up the coast, and the Russians on the other side of the continent.

He reported that Argentina hoped to do something about a base, and that Japan was interested in re-establishing their temporary base.

"But ours," he added, "is the only country flying planes to the Antarctic from 'The Outside,' and we help all the others."

Some of the others, especially the Russians, send most of their people and supplies by ship—including even some women.

This great continent, twice the size of the United States, is still largely unexplored. It is a place for young, hardy men, Lowell Thomas declares.

Few people realize how diverse is the work of a young polar scientist. Some study marine and land biology. Nearly all have a knowledge of geology, so essential to an understanding of Antarctica. Cosmic rays and ionospherics are common talk. Aerial photography is necessary to map the vast uncharted areas.

In charge of the scientific work at the time was twenty-nine-year-old tall, blond Bob Mason from Kansas.

Commander Paul Everett, a Navy flyer, has a most important assignment. He is in charge of all rescue operations and, in the vast area of low, low temperatures, that sometimes is no small or easy job. He gives one piece of advice to every man in Antarctica: Always be fully equipped. Wherever you go, be prepared to walk home.

Lowell Thomas heard much about the Seabees, the chaps who do the heavy construction work at the bases. For one thing, they put up the nuclear plant that supplies the power at Camp McMurdo. They also deserve credit for putting in the under-the-ice buildings at the South Pole. Here they work in temperatures around minus thirty, forty and even lower. The chaplain admires the men, and they have an affectionate regard for him. And this is a place of great tolerance. The McMurdo mess hall is open around the clock during the season here, where the so-called Antarctic summer lasts from September to April.

It was a thrilling experience for Lowell Thomas to fly, along with Navy friends and General Jimmy Doolittle, to the South Pole over a realm of ice where explorers had fought their slow and dangerous way from the Ross Sea shelf, into the mountains, and on across the high Antarctic plateau. What a contrast to the way it is done today.

Now they were making those eight hundred odd miles over icy mountains in less than three hours. It seemed fantastic. Naturally the talk was of the desperate attempts of early explorers to reach South Pole. Looking down on Beardmore Glacier and the Queen Maude Mountains, they thought of Shackleton and his men who almost reached the Pole on a Christmas Day, but had to turn back. They thought of the 1911 race for the ultimate South when Amundsen, the Norwegian, made it, and Scott, the Englishman, reached the Pole only to freeze to death on the return journey. Dogs and ponies, and even motor sledges could never compare with planes.

The scientists and their companions right at the bottom of the world came out from under the ice to greet them, and they soon learned that life at the Pole was indeed a life under the ice. There were eleven scientists and eleven Navy people living down in great tunnels cut deep in the ice. Although it was minus thirty-two above, down in the tunnels it was snug and warm. They were amazed at the comforts—the mess hall, the kitchen, laboratories, sick bay, and the living quarters. The South Pole residents assured their guests that thirty-two below was "Riviera weather." They told how a few months before they had seen the temperature drop to one hundred degrees below zero!

In his exciting life Lowell Thomas had experienced many thrilling adventures. But before leaving the

South Pole he had another novel and spectacular experience—riding in a Navy icebreaker, as it banged its way through the Ross Sea.

Let him tell it as it happened: "I have just come from the U. S. S. Glacier, our largest and most powerful icebreaker. Earlier explorers, Scott, Shackleton, Amundsen, Byrd, and all the rest, when they encountered ice four and five feet thick, were licked and had to wait for another season in the hope there would be less ice.

"You should see the U. S. S. Glacier bang its way through the frozen sea! As I stood in the bow, watching the great heavily plated ship ram into the ice, then slide up on it, then back off and go at it again, I wished I had a Cinerama camera and crew.

"The U. S. S. Glacier is three hundred and ten feet long, with a seventy-four foot beam, twenty-eight foot draft, with a carbon-tempered steel bow, and is driven by the largest diesel-electric propulsion plant on any ship in the world—**twenty-one thousand horsepower!** She carries a crew of twenty officers and two hundred and sixty men, nearly a million gallons of fuel, and sufficient supplies to stay at sea for a journey of twenty-five thousand miles. There is nowhere to get fuel down here in the Antarctic. Any icebreaker is liable to get caught in the ice, but the Glacier has its own way of avoiding the dilemma. In her hold she carries one hundred and forty thousand gallons of water, which, merely by the flip of a dial, can be shifted from one side of the ship to the other—to create a ten per cent artificial roll that enables her to break loose from the grip of the ice!

"Also, she can get up to full speed in a distance of three ship lengths. It's quite an experience to be on the Glacier as she backs up and then goes full speed ahead into ice against which an ordinary vessel wouldn't even make a dent. And this frozen Ross Sea through which we are crashing our way is larger than Texas. We now have men who are experts at looking down from a plane and picking the best route, which information they radio to the Glacier. Helicopters also assist in the scouting.

"When the icebreaker and a string of supply ships left New Zealand, the convoy had clear going for twelve hundred miles. After covering this in four days, it entered pack ice through which it pushed on for another seven hundred miles at the rate of a hundred miles a day. Upon reaching the Ross Sea, without the icebreaker Glacier there wouldn't have been any chance. Now for six days they have been ramming through this solid, heavy ice at about four miles a day, with only a week more to go, but now at no more than three miles a day. However, the important thing is that they will get through. These twenty-one thousand horses of the icebreaker Glacier won't be denied."

A few days later Lowell Thomas had flown off along the coast to get acquainted with the penguins. So amusing did they prove that he was reluctant to leave them. He called them nature's number one clowns, as they have so often been described by other penguin admirers.

The penguin visit began at a rookery where a colony of three or four thousand auks had congregated at Cape Royds, which was not only penguin headquarters but had been the base for the Shackleton and Scott expeditions on the Antarctic coast.

It was a unique experience to be able to visit the wooden huts once occupied by Scott and Shackleton which had only recently been reclaimed from the snow and ice and were found to be in much the same condition as when they were occupied. It is an unwritten law that visitors must not touch anything or take away a souvenir. There were blankets on the bunks, food on the stove, and supplies on the shelves. On the table there were notebooks, magazines, and newspapers. Even the men's Antarctic clothing was just where the earlier explorers had left it.

Here they visited with the British scientist and his assistant who were staying in the Shackleton hut while making a study of the Adelie penguin, the most numerous variety. From them they learned that there are seventeen different kinds of penguins in the Antarctic. The Adelie is the one usually seen in pictures, formal white shirt front, not over two feet tall. One familiar picture that brings laughter to grownups and children alike is a picture of the white-shirted penguin with his black "tails" plus a bow tie that some Seabee has slipped over his head. Since the penguin is unafraid of man, he can be most amusing.

The largest penguin, Lowell Thomas reminds us, is the Emperor, eight or nine times the size of the Adelie. But the Emperor is not so numerous as the Adelie.

This was the breeding season, and the visitor noted how busy the penguins were, either on their nests or waddling off in search of mates; how they paid little attention to him and scolded only if he stepped too close to their nests.

Obviously penguins are home lovers and fond of their frigid habitat. The young scientist told how he had taken banded penguins to another part of the Antarctic, several thousand miles away, and how the birds found their way back home through the heavy seas. Although they do not fly, they are excellent swimmers. It is exciting to see them leap onto the ice from the sea and waddle away.

The behavior of the penguin is one of the many studies being featured by the young scientists; this, along with biology, seismology, the earth's magnetic field and the aurora australis.

Lowell Thomas asked, did the mild and humorous penguin have any enemies? What does he live on in this desolate region of ice and snow? In reply, he heard how although there is no visible plant life on the land, the sea around the Antarctic continent is rich with plankton, a sort of weak seaweed on which small crustaceans feed. Fish and squid live on plankton, and these, in turn, are eaten by the penguin and the Antarctic seal.

The penguin, said the scientists, has only two enemies. One is the sea leopard and one is the killer whale. The killer whale is a fierce-looking creature with a large dorsal fin and a dolphin-like head. He is known as the demon of the Antarctic—not only ready to attack any penguin, but even to battle the sea leopard, and attack man himself.

The penguin seems not to mind low temperatures, even when it drops to a hundred degrees below zero. Then there is the wind that sweeps across the icy waste sometimes at a hundred miles an hour. So, the most comfortable place to be is under the ice, in those man-made tunnels. Antarctica sounds romantic, but it is one of the toughest assignments that man has found anywhere on our planet.

When you land in the Antarctic plateau, says Lowell Thomas, the first evidence you see of human habitation is gasoline drums, also a radio antenna or two, and some small wooden shafts through which you descend into the snow tunnels, at the South Pole, and at Byrd Station.

How are the snow tunnels made? They start out, as the Seabees explained, as trenches. These trenches are carved out of the closely packed snow by machines designed and built in Switzerland. Each machine weighs twenty tons and is powered by General Motors diesel engines and propelled by a system of hydraulic pumps and motors. These arrive by ship in sections and are assembled on the spot.

The whole setup is so ingenious, he says, that it has to be seen to be believed. These machines accomplish miracles. "With one you can cut a swathe nine feet wide, four feet deep, and three hundred feet long in half an hour; so each trench that becomes a tunnel is the result of a series of such cuts, the machine milling the snow and hurling it seventy feet or so in the air."

He goes on to say, "When the trench is from twenty-eight to thirty-six feet deep, the whole thing is covered over with eight-gauge galvanized iron segments, and snow is packed on top; so on the surface you can walk over a tunnel or drive a weasel over it and not know that it is there.

"Where a tunnel is only used for communication purposes—going from one area to another—it is a great circular metal tube, from fifteen to thirty-six feet in diameter.

"In the tunnels are wooden buildings, prefabricated structures, large enough so that each may have four or five room units, mess hall, offices, laboratories, sleeping quarters, and so on. These structures are shoved into the tunnels, several feet narrower than the tunnel, so there is room for a walkway on either side, a space that also keeps the heat in the buildings from melting the walls of the snow tunnels. For the same reason they are built several feet off the floor. One tunnel down here where I am runs for eighteen hundred feet—more than a third of a mile.

"The tunnel walls don't look like ice, and they are not. They are nothing more than layers of wind-blown snow, so packed that the texture is changed and it looks like neither ice nor snow. It looks more like white limestone. Glacier experts can tell the age of these layers and sometimes they bottle some from a 200 or 300-year-old layer."

The men actually live the year around down in the ice. Some of them go above and work in seventy below zero weather, but not for long. . . . One Seabee spoke of doing some surveying on the South Pole airstrip when it was one hundred and four below zero; he

Lowell Thomas and Tibetan school children

The Dalai Lama's sister, Lowell Thomas and Tibetan children

Admiral James Reedy, Lowell Thomas and Rear Admiral David M. Tyree, U.S.N. (Ret.), at the South Pole in the winter of 1962.

Lowell Thomas, Jr. and Lowell Thomas, Sr. while flying over the North Pole.

worked until the transit froze up. The lowest recorded record, he said, was one hundred and forty-five!

On occasion they all emerged from below: Such an occasion was the arrival of the Commerce Secretary Hodges-General Doolittle-Lowell Thomas party. They were all mainly excited over greeting the legendary airman who bombed Tokyo. Although only forty below that day, the men at the Pole wore heavy face-covering parkas and long fur gloves.

A stay in the Antarctic is a lonely experience, but the men do have their amusements. To break the monotony, one way is to get in touch with amateur radio operators all over the world. Occasionally a new motion picture film arrives, and when they haven't a new one, they run an old one. In fact, they run it and rerun it; and often even run it backwards. Sometimes they see a film so many times they know the dialogue by heart. Then they run it with the sound off and substitute their own dialogue. As Mr. Thomas puts it, "dialogue that would curl the hair of the men who wrote the script."

Like soldiers in wartime, their humor also runs to pin-ups. After a hard-bitten Admiral was shocked and demanded a reform, the boys figured out a dodge. Now they hang frames with pictures on both sides, one side showing scenery or a patriotic theme, the other girls, girls, girls! Although they will do anything for a laugh at the South Pole, Lowell Thomas says, "They are dedicated fellows, doing an important work for their country, nearly all in the interest of pure science . . . and I take my fur cap off to all of them as I say, SO LONG TO THE SOUTH POLE!"

Returning from another round-the-world trip following his Polar adventure, he spent Christmas with his family in Hawaii and seemed content to settle down for awhile. But it didn't last long. The exciting journey he had just finished, the South Pole expedition with the Navy, the stop-off in India to see Prime Minister Nehru and even more exciting, the meeting with the Dalai Lama at Dharamsala, followed by a visit to the Shah of Persia, all this was behind him. But something new and most unusual lay ahead. This time it was a surprise invitation to hurry out to New Guinea for an adventure with the Stone Age people of the world's wildest island.

Through the famous Dr. Charles Mayo of the Mayo Clinic he heard from the Mt. Hagen District Commissioner and others that they wanted him to attend a special and strange ceremony honoring the Governor General of Australia. This was something his wanderlust spirit could appreciate—and off he went. With him went a film crew, including a director who had worked with him on Cinerama.

New Guinea, the last home of the Stone Age people, had long fascinated Lowell Thomas. Naked men coming out of the bush by the tens of thousands, carrying spears and stone axes, speaking only the dialect of their own tribe, with bones in their noses and holding high their axes of obsidian, sharp enough to shave with. For coinage they used shells of mother-of-pearl. And there were two million of them living in the eastern half of an island that from end to end is as far as it is from Boston to Kansas City, or from Chicago to Los Angeles. They subsisted mainly on sweet potatoes, some as large as our pumpkins, plus small game, fish and wild fruit. They were strong, bronze in coloring, and wore fabulous headdresses for their celebrations.

The headdresses were worth a fortune, for they were contrived from the feathers of the rare bird of paradise and the black tails of the cassowary. The shimmering, shaking headdresses with the exquisite priceless feathers was to be an unforgettable sight.

On the main day of the celebration, these Stone Age men who did not even know that other continents existed and many who had never seen a white man, came singing and shouting, nearly a hundred thousand of them, naked bodies painted—and all moving, row upon row in rhythm. They had enjoyed stimulants and food, and they had long been cannibalistic. But now—in this new age for them, would there be a feeling of what District Commissioner Tom Ellis dreamed — a day when they would form a new nation? For centuries they had all been enemies. Could they now become friendly and learn to understand each other and form a common government? That question is still to be answered.

They might enjoy the gold that could be found in the rushing streams. In time, more and more great coffee plantations would be created with the rich soil of their huge island. As for Lowell Thomas, he would never again, perhaps, enjoy a greater adventure than this visit to the Stone Age people of a long lost world.

Chapter Twenty-two

The Fabulous Fireplace

Lowell Thomas, having been brought up on geology, archaeology, and history, has never lost his special interest in stones. His boyhood home in Victor, Colorado, the rich gold-mining town inside the rim of an extinct volcano, remained vivid in his memory, where at an altitude of some ten thousand feet the sun, as he described it, "dropped each night like fire behind the rugged Sangre de Cristo (Blood of Christ) Range and the stars hung close to us like lanterns." Here the daily conversation had been of rocks, of trachyte, phonolite, and especially gold-bearing sylvanite and clavorite.

The wide world into which his travels carried him was a world of rocks and minerals, and out of them men had constructed wonders as marvelous as those of nature. In his many wanderings, he had been able to trace the civilization created by man over many centuries.

And from this had come an idea that finally materialized. Today a huge fireplace made up of stones that in a way tells the history of mankind. When he suggested this to his wife, she said she certainly didn't want any such a fireplace in their Georgian home. She wanted a home, not a museum. Of course she was right. He realized that.

But he had taken an old barn and transformed it into a community center for his Quaker Hill neighborhood. Coming in from the golf links that stretched into the rolling countryside beyond the farm, the fireplace blazing six-foot logs would not be out of place.

For the inscription on the lintel, carved into the stone in Sanskrit, he used the following Sanskrit proverb: "One who lets his day pass without practicing generosity or enjoying life's pleasures—is like a blacksmith's bellows—he breathes but he does not live."

The giant fireplace, rising from the floor of the barn to the rafters, is faced with two hundred and twenty cement blocks, each a foot square. The plan, which over the years he has carried out, was to remove each block as the appropriate stone arrived. First, out went requests by letter; also a message by radio, to friends in distant lands; to explorers, archaeologists, diplomats, missionaries, soldiers, and other travelers. By short wave came replies and promises all the way from the Polar Seas north of Greenland in the Arctic to unexplored Palmer Land in the Antarctic. An article in "This Week Magazine" also brought fast and startling results, including a part of the Washington Monument.

At the bottom on one side of the fireplace there were several rows for prehistoric man; on the other side for the civilization of known man from five thousand years ago from the days of Ur and Babylon and Karnak. Also one row at the top was even left for the future.

One early contribution was a fragment of limestone from the palace of Sargon II (about 700 B.C.) at Khorsabad near Mosul on the upper Tigris. On the face of it had been inscribed some cuneiform characters in Assyrian. Dr. John Wilson of the University of Chicago Museum explained how museums could not give away any of their possessions, however, he was impressed and they could loan an antiquity. So in this instance he wanted his friend Lowell Thomas to have the Sargon stone for the fireplace. Whereupon he drew up papers loaning it to Lowell Thomas for a period of one thousand years.

Then from the oldest city in the world came a brick bearing the stamped inscription of King Ishme Dagon of Ur of the Chaldees. This gift came from the University of Pennsylvania Museum whose scientists had secured it while on a joint expedition with scientists from Oxford.

Set next to it is a large square brick with a strip of cuneiform writing across the middle, from Babylon, of the time of Nebuchadnezzar. And beside it is a stone from Mount Ararat that Lowell, Jr. brought home from a remote part of Turkey, from the actual spot on which the Ark ran aground, said young Lowell.

"How come you can get these stones?" guests are always asking.

Lowell Thomas explains: "Restoration work is constantly going on in connection with any important ancient ruin. A broken piece must be replaced of course. It is best to work with museums and expeditions. There was one expedition, for example, led by Dr. Nelson Glueck of Yale, that uncovered Ezion-Gerber, King Solomon's seaport at the head of the Gulf of Akaba in western Asia." This fabulous fireplace boasts stones from one of the furnaces at Ezion-Geber where were smelted the ores from King Solomon's mines.

No such record of man's achievement would be complete without a stone from the Great Wall of China. A block part way up on the left side came from the Great Wall, that famous defense of over a thousand miles set up in the third century B.C. between Mongolia and China proper by Emperor Shih Hwang-ti to keep out the barbarians.

When Explorer Henry Field gave a stone lamp, he said, "It may have been by the light of this lamp that some Cro-Magnon artist drew a saber-toothed tiger on the walls of his cave twenty-five thousand years ago."

From Japan came a stone from the ruins of Emperor Hirohito's palace in Tokyo. From General Stratemeyer, MacArthur's air commander in Japan, there arrived later a group of stones from Hiroshima and Nagasaki, the cities destroyed by the atom bomb.

One radio broadcast was heard in a number of far-off places, and a Peruvian expedition in one of the inner valleys, a valley between the ranges of the Andes, sent word they would like to send a stone from a pre-Inca city where they were working, and they did!

Robert L. (Believe-it-or-not) Ripley brought back from his travels a weird Mayan image and a carved block from one of the jungle-covered cities of Central America. It was Colonel Edwin C. Cooper, ace war photographer of World War I, who supplied the Inca stone from Cuzco, the once spectacular capital of the great Inca empire. Dr. Herbert Spinden of the Brooklyn Museum presented a flat stone from Zuni, one of the fabled Seven Cities of Cibola—and so on and on.

A priest from Puerto Rico sent a strip of marble that he explained had come from the Basilica of St. Peter's in Rome.

A few of the stones have their own special beauty, such as the piece of marble brought from Korea by Air Force Captain Augustus Theodore. It is a marble head of Buddha and the only word that describes it is **glorious.** How did it happen that a statue of Buddha showed Greek influence, Lowell Thomas wanted to know. When Dr. William Hung from Harvard and the University of Peking came to visit, he gave an explanation.

When the armies of Alexander the Great marched across Persia into Afghanistan and India over two thousand years ago, they left their mark on all the countries they touched, and in the course of centuries Grecian culture continued to spread on and on until it crossed China, and even reached Korea.

For our period there are stones from the opposite ends of the earth. In the row next to the top there are stones from near the North Pole and the South Pole. Captain Bob Bartlett of North Pole fame brought back a stone from the Peary Monument which is on a fifteen-hundred-foot promontory at the tip of Cape York looking out across the Polar Sea.

U. S. Navy Captain Finn Ronne boxed a stone from Palmer Land on the Antarctic ice cap and, since the party had to leave in a small plane, the stone had to be left behind. Two years went by. Organizing another expedition, Commander Ronne revisited Palmer Land, picked up the box, and finally delivered it to Quaker Hill.

There are granite and sandstone blocks from many places familiar to Americans—a tile from Jamestown, the first English settlement in America, a brick from Williamsburg, and a fragment from Plymouth Rock, along with rocks from Mount Vernon, the White House, the Washington Monument, the Gatun Lock of the Panama Canal, the core of the Grand Coulee Dam, and from one of the pylons of the Golden Gate Bridge.

Alfred E. Smith, former Governor of New York, sent a slab of marble from the world's tallest building, the Empire State Building. Other famous New York buildings called for representation. There is a square stone from Radio City, given by the Rockefellers, and a gargoyle from St. Patrick's Cathedral, a gift from Cardinal Spellman.

From time to time stones arrived from all over the British Empire. From Ireland came a stone from the Dominican Priory at Roscommon, erected by O'Connor, King of Connaught in the thirteenth century. . . . An impressive souvenir of "The London Blitz" is a stone from the Houses of Parliament, the original Hall of Rufus, nine hundred years old, also one from the dome of St. Paul's.

Many unique gifts were from ancient sites. Commander Donald MacMillan sent a stone from the ruins of the home of Eric the Red in Greenland. One friend brought part of the Great Pyramid of Cheops, and others came from Ninevah, Ephesus, Carthage, and, of course, the Acropolis at Athens. There is even a part of a statue from the Forum in Rome, and one, of magnificent pink marble from the romantic North African marble city of Sabratha. Lowell, Jr. brought home stones from St. Sophia in Istanbul and from the unexplored heart of the desert Rub al Khali.

Jerusalem would have to be there. An almost unbelievable gift came from Colonel John Whiting and Mrs. Bertha Spafford Vester who were leaders of the famous American colony in Jerusalem. They shipped Lowell Thomas a part of the walls of ancient Jericho and a section of a priceless fluted column from the church of the Holy Sepulchre. The gift was made possible because this most important Christian shrine had been and still is undergoing repairs. Part of the dome and some of the pillars had given way. Now in this fabulous fireplace you can see a portion of the original church. Lowell Thomas points out how engineers are unable to explain the fluting, so perfectly done, nearly two thousand years ago.

Writer and commentator Henry J. Taylor, while in Egypt and Libya with Montgomery's army, was lucky enough to secure a stone that had been knocked loose from the Great Pyramid at Giza. Stricken with a virulent form of malaria, he had to be rushed home. Although he became delirious as he lay in the tail of the Air Force bomber, he did not forget the stone. As a matter of fact, he carried it beside him on the stretcher.

All travelers agree that the most beautiful building in the world created by man is the Taj Mahal, the tomb of pure white marble erected on the bank of the River Jumna. And nearly everybody knows the story of how the Mogul Emperor, Shah Jehan, built it in memory of his beloved Persian Queen, Mumtaz Mahal. . . . How could a stone from this priceless jewel of a building reach Quaker Hill? The answer is simple. The building was undergoing repairs when an Air Force colonel managed to get a large piece for Lowell Thomas.

The weird figure of a stone man, a mysterious statue, was brought by Captain Irving Johnson of "The Yankee" sailing ship, from far-off Easter Island, most remote island in the world.

Of course the father and son travelers brought a stone from Lhasa in Tibet, a mani stone, from a prayer wall. It came from the Potala, the great, gold-roofed palace of the Dalai Lama, now despoiled by the Chinese Reds.

The carving on the stone is the Lamaist prayer uttered millions of times a day in Tibet—

OM MANI PADME HUM

Former President Herbert Hoover made one somber and one humorous contribution. With his traveling companion, Ambassador Hugh Gibson, he turned in a fragment from the Reichschancellory in Berlin and another from the subterranean bunker where Hitler and Eva Braun were married and then did away with themselves. And then the ex-President who was once a geologist and mining engineer, suggested one stone for the fireplace that is only indirectly connected with Man. At a special ceremony he made a witty speech, telling how right there on Quaker Hill he had found a part of the original crust of the Earth. He said he thought the planet itself should be represented. So, there in one of the lower corners of the fireplace is the block of gneiss presented by Herbert Hoover.

Chapter Twenty-three

Hammersley Hill

All during the years of struggle and early successes, Lowell Thomas had dreamed of a spacious home somewhere in the country. But even he, for all his vision, could hardly have dreamed of so handsome an estate as Hammersley Hill where he and his wife now live. In fact, this had been another man's dream.

The man, Fred F. French, who, during the 1920's had made a fortune building skyscrapers in New York City. At the height of his financial success he had created a baronial estate worthy of his grandiose accomplishments. It was after World War I that he found a site that suited his ideas of a sort of American princeliness, and for a time it looked as though he might live like a storybook king.

The place he found was in an area of forests and farms some seventy-five miles north of New York City, near the Connecticut line, in the Berkshire Hills. On the maps it was called Quaker Hill. It was really a ridge and a plateau, eleven or twelve miles long. In the middle of it stood an old weathered meeting house across the road from a cemetery where Revolutionary heroes had been buried. Nearby is this plaque:

> OBLONG MEETING HOUSE
> of the Society of Friends
> Erected in 1742 South of the Road
> Present building erected in 1764
> First effective action against slavery
> taken here in 1767.
> Occupied as Hospital January 1779
> by Revolutionary Soldiers.
> Many of them are buried south of
> the road.
> Meeting divided 1828
> Meetings ceased in this House 1885.

It was said that both General Washington and General Burgoyne attended services in this meeting house.

The builder of skyscrapers, the engineer from New York, was more interested in the view than in the historic background. He quietly bought up some thousand acres of the high land, later tearing down nearly all the farmhouses and barns, and planting long rows of Norway spruce and pine, a man-made forest of evergreen trees where there long had been open fields. Nearly a million trees he planted that today are full grown, for that was nearly forty years ago. The Berkshire hills in October were a tapestry of color, and there was a purple haze in the Catskills beyond. At the same time he planned and built a vast Georgian house with thirty-two rooms and fourteen bathrooms. To obtain the faint pinkish look of ancient brick he had a special kiln built. The house alone, forty years ago, is said to have cost him some $400,000. Proudly he surveyed his acres and acres of green lawns, his sparkling pond in the yard and two beautiful lakes.

A sad fate awaited him. He went broke during the "Great Crash," and a short time afterward died of a heart attack. The fine house and vast estate and beautiful lakes were put up for sale.

In a time of depression who would buy such a place? It would take a fortune to handle the three thousand acres, the fabulous house, the immense grounds, and the lakes and ponds. To make such changes as a new owner might desire and to furnish it would also require a staggering sum. Beyond that, the cost of maintenance, what of that?

Who would have courage enough, even though he were wealthy, to take on the burden of such a baronial estate? Surely it would have to be somebody who had made a fortune and kept it, or someone sure of a large regular income in the years ahead.

Now Lowell Thomas had never plunged in the market, had never drilled an oil well, had never built a skyscraper, had never found a gold mine. True, he had used a pick and shovel, but the real gold he had unearthed during his life was not the yellow metal he had known in Colorado. However, he was bold—perhaps reckless.

However, he had proved, as few others have, that a man can become well off just by talking and writing. In fact, he already had made and lost several good-sized fortunes. One of these was on his speaking tour of the world. Later he did it again with radio, also with Cinerama. He had helped in the making of some thousands of motion pictures. He had written many books such as his "Lawrence of Arabia," and another on Count von Luckner. He also had for years been the voice of Fox Movietone. But he had always said he was not a businessman and knew nothing about money.

At any rate, soon after Fred French died he boldly took over the French domain, and a few years later the move was made from their beautiful home two miles away at Clover Brook. Now, at Hammersley Hill, his wife lightened and brightened the dark paneled rooms and had a graceful stairway built to the second floor. It was her artistic touches that gave the inside of the house the elegance that the architect had given the outside, with its soft red bricks, green shutters and white enamel trim.

Her spirit filled the house with a wonderful radiance. Always an incomparable hostess, she welcomed the innumerable guests that arrived endlessly, for week ends or long visits. Lowell was forever inviting people, though he was no help as a mechanic around the house. It always amused her that he had two blind spots, mechanics and finances.

Lowell, Jr. tells an amusing incident to illustrate his father's lack of mechanical ability. He was only six years old at the time. His father was taking him for a ride over the winding roads of Quaker Hill in an old red Marquette convertible.

The senior Thomas had the accelerator down to the floor. It got stuck and he said: "What do we do now?" Whereupon his much more practical son who later became a famous airman and world traveler, just reached and turned off the ignition.

In spite of all that he earns, finance is a puzzle to Lowell Thomas. He leaves all money matters to his colleague, Frank Smith, who is known as a financial wizard, and who says of him, "Lowell is a soft touch. He'll give help to anyone who needs money. I would say that his primary characteristic is his absolute unselfishness, his kindness, and his consideration for other people. He just can't see anyone hurt or insulted or slighted or without something interesting to do." Then Frank Smith goes on to tell of the pearl diver from the South Seas whose medical bills he paid, and of countless others whose burdens he eased.

Hammersley Hill, as they renamed it, once the Thomases took over, became a mecca for visitors. Week ends proved lively but, at the same time, restful.

Herbert Hoover said, "I've always been impressed with the peaceful, kind dignity of the Frances Thomas household and the warm, stimulating group of friends they nearly always have around."

Dr. Stinchfield called Lowell Thomas Mister International. Of Hammersley Hill he said, "At his home one week will be the top skier from Austria or Norway. The next week it will be the foreign minister from Indo-China; then the fellow who knows how to make the best whistle for ducks. He plays absolutely no favorites. He's so interested in everything that he can't limit himself to one group."

Sir Hugh Stott Taylor says of his Princeton days

that he always knew everybody and never had to ask a name twice. He told me that: "He had a voracious appetite for getting to know people and still does. That's part of his skill."

In spite of an always crowded schedule, Lowell Thomas finds time to play. Nearly everybody has heard of The Nine Old Men, his famous softball team, with its special stadium on Quaker Hill.

In the 1930's, Lowell Thomas enrolled friends and neighbors in a team, first known as The Debtors and Creditors. Later, when they became involved in spirited battles with a team of White House Cabinet officers, correspondents and secret servicemen organized by President Franklin D. Roosevelt, the team was renamed The Nine Old Men.

The names of the nine old men who opposed the Roosevelt team are an imposing list: General Ted Roosevelt, Lanny Ross, Colonel Stoopnagle, Paul Webb, Jimmy Doolittle, Frank Hawks, Believe-it-or-not Ripley, James Melton, Dale Carnegie, Gene Tunney, Ted Shane, Monroe Leaf, and such legendary baseball heroes as Walter Johnson and Babe Ruth.

Sometimes the games played by celebrities had purposes other than to enjoy softball.

Judge Murphy tells of one instance that stands out for pure inspiration above all others. He says, "During the war Trinity Pawling School was devoted to the rehabilitation of shell-shocked aviators. Eddie Rickenbacker had gone through his terrific ordeal in the Pacific and had been so badly wounded that his legs were like rusty springs."

Lowell Thomas arranged to have him pitch for his team as an inspiration to the airmen who were recuperating nearby.

Here are Judge Murphy's recollections:

"Eddie Rickenbacker pitched a full game of ball. It was one of the most remarkable demonstrations of courage and stamina that I have ever seen. Although he was suffering all the time, he wouldn't give up because all these boys were in the bleachers cheering everything he did. The medical colonel in charge told me afterwards that there was no tonic or inspiration those boys received that equalled Eddie Rickenbacker's exhibition. And Lowell Thomas was responsible for it."

Although he had built a fine golf course for the community, he wound up with a second one, on his own property, one he says just came into existence by accident. And on this Hammersley Hill course some rather impressive guests have played. Taking one special day as a sample of the variety of talent he so often assembles, here is one card:

Robert Trent Jones, Golf Architect

Joe Kirkwood from Australia

Frank M. Smith, Financier

Edward R. Murrow, Commentator

Sam Snead

Francis Ouimet

Gene Sarazen

George Ferrier, Golf Pro from Scotland

Johnny Farrell, from Baltusrol

Fred Bantz, Navy Undersecretary
Willie Turnesa, Golf Pro
Carl T. Hogan, Golf Star
Bill Goldbeck, Mount Kisco Country Club Pro
Thomas E. Dewey, former Governor of New York

These, and others like them have played here.

Paul O'Neil has made an attempt to explain Lowell Thomas in Sports Illustrated, for few men own private golf courses. He says, "The L. T. course came as an afterthought in a life devoted to achieving simple princeliness and is so mixed up in his mind with other projects that he tends to classify it with his softball diamond, his local ski tow, his international fireplace (stones from all parts of the world), his stand of small dawn sequoias (from deepest Yunan Province) and, at times (while on expeditions), to forget all about it."

The acres and acres of lawns around their home seemed a natural, though it took men, machinery, and money to shape it up.

Already, right at his very door was what most people would consider a fairly good green. But he had a New Hampshire firm truck in rolled-up pregrown greens, and in no time at all, the Hammersley Hill Golf and Hunt Club was there.

The word "hunt" is on the scorecard because there are so many over-water-holes and trees. It includes what he calls the shortest hole in the world, eighty yards. Also he laid out the longest, almost half a mile from tee to green, 800 yards, par 7. Now he and his friends could play either nine or twelve holes. The shorter one he called the Vice Presidential course and the second, the Presidential course, to commemorate the visits of both General Ike and Dick Nixon to Quaker Hill.

Many have asked why their home is called Hammersley Hill. The explanation is that for two hundred years the property, together with Quaker Lake and some fifteen hundred acres that he gave to the community, belonged to the Hammersleys, an English family to whom it was given as a grant by Queen Anne in early Colonial days. In fact, the Hammersleys continued to own it until 1928 when it was taken over by the builder of skyscrapers, Fred F. French. Then L. T. took it over to keep it from being broken up and sold in lots as a subdivision, a thing that would have changed the entire Quaker Hill region.

A friend of the family says, "Frances Thomas can have a party of fifty people arranged and an hour before the guests arrive receive a call from Lowell saying he is leaving for South America or has an emergency call to go to Africa. She knows this is in his blood and there is no reason to stop him. 'That's fine, Tommy,' she'll say. 'Go right ahead. Maybe I'll join you!' "

And that's just about how they live. Here today, and where under the sun will they be tomorrow?

As for the more serious side of life, he taught his son that goodness can be expressed in a mine tunnel as well as in a church. The family attends a nondenominational church on Quaker Hill where, as he puts it, "Everybody goes!" A wealthy Quaker long ago gave money for a meeting house on Quaker Hill with the proviso that it was to be nondenominational. And because it bears no denominational label, the church has endeared itself in the community so that people of any faith, as well as people of no professed faith at all, attend regularly.

Chapter Twenty-four

Lowell Thomas at Home

Mildred Comfort speaking: Last fall Lowell Thomas was at home—perhaps an unusual place for this world traveler and adventurer to be—but here he was in his country home, known as Hammersley Hill, and I was his guest. Out of a blue sky had come the invitation for me to go to New York and spend a week or so on the three-thousand-acre estate near Pawling. There I was to become acquainted with the subject of my assignment from T. S. Denison & Co., Inc., for the "Men of Achievement" series. Even before receiving this unusual invitation, I had tentatively titled the manuscript "Lowell Thomas, Adventurer," and I have never since had occasion to change the wording.

"The trip and all as my guest" read the invitation, and Lowell Thomas meant it literally. I flew to New York, landed at Idlewild Airport and was ensconced—the proper word—in the Waldorf Astoria. No sooner had I been settled in comfortably than the telephone rang and I remember thinking, "These big hotels are always concerned over any special desire of a new guest." But it was not the desk calling, but Mary Davis, Mr. Thomas' Radio City secretary who had arranged my trip. She said, "Mr. Thomas is on the line waiting to talk to you."

Then came that well-known voice saying, "Good evening, Mrs. Comfort," and I was saying, "Good evening, Mr. Thomas."

Was I taken care of? Did I wish to drive out to Pawling in the morning? Or did I prefer to take the train? If I wished to drive, he would send a car for me. I said maybe I should see Grand Central Station (since I had always come in to the Penn Station) and that I also wanted to ride on a commuters' train. He said all right, but warned me that the best train left rather early, at eight o'clock.

Grand Central, after the Waldorf-Astoria, did not seem quite as grand as I had expected. But the ride into the country was interesting. So were the passengers, reading their papers or absorbed in the contents of their brief cases.

I would be "met," Mr. Thomas had said. And who should meet me but Mrs. Thomas herself! The moment I saw her I felt the warmth of her welcome. She was a striking woman with a gracious manner, and I noted the purple tinge of her hair, the blue of her eyes, and the freshness of her skin. She took my heavy suitcase, leaving the light bag for me, then introduced me to her woman passenger, a young girl from the British Embassy just back from the Sudan. In her light-blue Cadillac we drove home.

The great house came in view as we rounded a

L. to r.: Col. Bernt Balchen, first to pilot a plane over both North and South Poles; Adm. Donald B. MacMillan, 87 years old and the only living member of the Peary expedition—first to reach the North Pole; Lowell Thomas, Sr. and Lowell Thomas, Jr. and Sir Hubert Wilkins photographed in an Air Force plane as it circled the North Pole.

Lowell Thomas interviews Prime Minister Nehru.

Hammersley Hill, home of Lowell Thomas.

Lowell Thomas with General Douglas MacArthur

curved driveway, a rose-brick house with green blinds, dazzling white trim, and surroundings of wide green lawns sloping to gardens and a pool-like lake where later I was to see wild deer coming down to drink. The Georgian colonial architecture gave it all a homey yet elegant appearance.

The two dogs, Kum Kum, a grayish hair-faced dog that reminded me of our sheep dogs in Wyoming, and Jaques, a perfectly groomed French poodle, every hair in his topknot in place, came barking to welcome us. A butler, Henning, took my luggage and showed me up to my room. Mrs. Thomas had given me what she still calls her son's room, although he, by the way, while I was there, called from Alaska where he lives and said, "Now that I'm thirty-nine, let's forget the 'Sonny,' how about it?" The story of the son's life would fill an exciting book. For he also has been everywhere and today is one of the most influential and best-known figures in Alaska.

That first week end was a gay, social delight—and no work. There was a golf match on when I arrived, with guests from England who had flown over for a tournament. We watched the play for awhile, and Mr. Thomas came across the course to greet me. Lunch was served at The Barn. (It really was a barn that had been built by Quakers and the Thomases had turned it into a community center.) It was here I first saw the fabulous fireplace that told the story of mankind. The distinguished guests who were being entertained included an English lord, and a former governor of New York, Mr. Dewey, who has a large farm in the neighborhood. The buffet lunch was just right, both the food and the talk. Later, in the afternoon, we returned to the big house for afternoon tea.

Guests also had come in from Australia, a father and teen-age son. The man, Edward Connellan of Alice Springs, right at the geographical center of their continent, runs one of the most important airlines of the Southern Hemisphere, and also owns a cattle ranch twice as big as the famed King Ranch in Texas. He had brought his son Roger along for the experience of buying planes in America, England and also in India. They both spoke with an "outback" accent, and how they did enjoy the tea, served from the lovely silver service! True Aussies, they balanced their fragile china cups and partook of the toasted scones and cookies. The exciting conversation turned to the Lassiter case, a mystery Lowell Thomas on a visit to Australia had helped to solve after it had puzzled Australia for a quarter of a century.

In the evening we were all invited to dinner at the Ducases who now live at Clover Brook, the original Lowell Thomas home on Quaker Hill. I remember best the great bouquets of chrysanthemums and Easter lilies along with the fifty guests and the delicious roast beef dinner. Later on we all drove back to The Barn to find logs blazing in the fabulous fireplace. There was music, much good talk, and a great deal of laughter, especially when Mr. Thomas had to interpret the Connellan speech, so different from our own brand of English.

On Sunday morning we all went to church. The little nondenominational white church standing near golden-leaved trees on a gentle slope with a view, through the clear glass windows, of the hills, was filled with neighbors. The services were simple—several hymns, a Bible reading, the Lord's Prayer, and a brief sermon. The week before, a Quaker had led the services. On this particular Sunday the guest preacher was Dr. Elfan Rees, a Welchman from the World Council of Churches in Geneva, whose books had been published by the Carnegie Foundation for International Peace. His sermon topic, naturally, was world peace.

The Cortland Linders, a shipping family, had us for luncheon, and we carried our trays out on a terrace that overlooked a deep valley in which gleamed two blue lakes, the one in the distance, the deep glacial lake that Frances and Lowell had given to the community as a part of a permanent park. The other they still own.

This was all wonderful entertainment and relaxation, but when would I get any work done? I need not have worried, for by Monday morning the house guests were gone and I was alone in the big house with the Thomases. A different atmosphere pervaded the place, for the working week had begun. Quantities of mail delivered in the library, my favorite room with its rich dark woodwork, its walls of books, comfortable chairs, a desk that had once belonged to the Duke of Wellington, reading lamps, and silken curtains through which the sun poured! Mr. Thomas had begun his labors early in the morning and I did not see him again until time for his broadcast at 6:45.

Each evening of my stay I sat opposite him in his broadcasting room in the studio—and when I say studio, I do not mean a single room. This studio on the lawn not far from the house is a large, two-story white frame building with garage space. On the first floor are the secretary and engineers' quarters, a radio studio and film-cutting room, a conference room, graced by a delightful wood-burning fireplace. On the second floor are the finance quarters and filing room, plus a small auditorium where programs may be tried out and where a hundred or more people may be seated.

The reason for building the studio is due to Lowell Thomas' consideration for other people. When he did his broadcasting in New York City, the Grand Central held the evening train "until Mr. Thomas is on board." To avoid this inconvenience to riders, he decided to build his own studio at home and broadcast from there. Also he found it more convenient and less tiring than the five-day-a-week trip into the city and back. Actually, he has had three different radio studios on Quaker Hill.

Behind him in his broadcasting room there is a map of the world, rising from the floor to the second-story ceiling. It is said to be the largest accurate hand-made map in the world, and was the work of Rand McNally's cartographers.

Several minutes before the broadcast he would be at his desk, the microphone in place. I would watch him as he hurriedly checked his manuscript, doing the final editing like any writer—scratching out a word or a line, setting in another choice to improve materials he had worked on during the afternoon right up to the very last moment. Only a professional writer could realize how much work goes into the short broadcast that begins so casually with "Good evening, everybody!" He had read newspapers, secured facts over teletype and telephone, perhaps had glanced through a half dozen books, conferred and consulted with experts or authorities, and had then the final work of composition. By the time he said "So long until tomorrow," he had achieved a smooth, conversational masterpiece of condensed news—usually ending on a note of humor. Sometimes his secretary reminded him, "Remember, boss, this time make it "So long until Monday!" And he would nod, and maybe forget and say "Tomorrow."

Speaking of secretaries, Lowell Thomas finds them indispensable. He has four of the most loyal, enthusiastic, hard-working secretaries in this country. First of all, there is Mary Davis in Rockefeller Center in New York, who, with Ann St. Peter, handles the main office—which is big business, for Lowell Thomas is more than a news commentator. His interests extend from Cinerama to book publishing and into many other fields. From New York he goes off on various expeditions and Mary Davis must make the arrangements. His secretaries must be people of taste, diplomacy, and ability—and they have ineffable charm. Back at the studio is the irreplaceable Electra and her engineer husband Gene. Electra, like the others, has been with him for years and years, but she retains her youthful enthusiasm and interest in everything. She is always on hand for the broadcasts, sitting at the desk with her boss, and, when necessary, remaining at the telephone for any last-minute news of importance.

Lowell Thomas had had a long list of engineers over

the years, until finally there was one in whom Electra showed a special interest. When they married, their boss gave them a house up the road for a wedding present, and there are now two sons who also are much interested in all the excitement and adventure that surrounds their parents.

On the second floor Dorothy Weigel writes checks and, under the instruction of Frank M. Smith, handles the finances of the entire menage. She is a pretty girl with a builder husband and children, and she says her own boss is a truly "big man," indeed a financial genius. Frank Smith, short, dynamic and good looking, seems more like a movie actor.

In the background, but also important, are John Zabbia and Irv Fleury. John is the caretaker of the archives and can put his hand on any book or paper, or reel of film anyone asks for. And it's quite a library to attend to, some eleven thousand volumes. He is a quiet man, gentle and obliging, just the type anybody would like to find in a library, although years ago he was a deep sea sailor from the Dalmation Coast. Irv is the Vermonter who runs the estate, the golf course, and everything out of doors.

Even though he is no longer with Lowell Thomas—he died while a guest in the big house—I feel another should be mentioned. Everybody I met on my visit talked of Prosper Buranelli who, they said, was a walking encyclopedia and a phenomenon in other ways. Lowell Thomas could ask him almost anything, about science, history, art, or politics, and he had the answers. They said he was as broad physically as he was mentally, and they all loved him. He had been with his friend for some thirty years.

People ask me if Lowell Thomas is as handsome as his pictures, or are they touched up? He is a slender, well-groomed, dynamic person. His thick, dark hair is barely touched with frost. His eyes are unusually bright blue, and he does not wear glasses. His habits are moderate and he is not fussy about food. Otherwise, he could not so easily adapt to foods of various nations. He does not smoke, except for a cigar now and then. He seldom drinks, though he may have a glass of wine or a highball before dinner. Indeed, he has an aversion to alcohol that goes back to his gold mining days when he saw what havoc it wrought among his Cripple Creek neighbors. Like all good travelers he is not critical of other people's habits.

His vanities are small ones. One day when I saw him wearing a big straw hat woven in an odd pattern, I remarked about it. He was on his way to the studio. Mrs. Thomas said, "Tommy, tell Mrs. Comfort how many hats you have."

"A hundred—maybe two hundred," he said and laughed. He collects hats unintentionally.

Due to Mrs. Thomas' fine direction, the household ran smoothly. I had breakfast in my room, and at one o'clock I lunched with Mrs. Thomas in the library. She always planned something she thought a Midwesterner might enjoy—lobster, crab, or fresh mushrooms from one of the nearby golf fairways. Late in the afternoon she would take me for a drive around The Hill. One afternoon I told her how, as children, we drove through the Minnesota woods in my father's horse-drawn delivery wagon, and how he would slow down so we could climb off the wagon seat and pick branches of autumn leaves. She asked, "Would you like to do that now?"

I said I would indeed. She'd stop the car and I'd pick a few branches of golden leaves. We'd drive on, exclaiming over the brilliant maples ahead and I'd gather more. We came home, the car filled with the loveliest autumn foliage I had seen since I was a child. It was she who gathered it all up and gave it to me in a vase to take up to my room. When Lily brought my breakfast tray the next morning, she exclaimed: "I never knew before that a bouquet of leaves could be as beautiful as flowers."

And speaking of trays, I thought I had seldom seen such beautiful china as that on my breakfast tray, delicate white china with a floral touch here and there. One day Mrs. Thomas told me about a dinner party to which she was invited during the Eisenhower administration. The occasion was a state dinner for the king and queen of Nepal whom Lowell knew. Her dinner partner was Dr. Charles Mayo of Minnesota who, in his gay, frank fashion informed her that he had rented his evening clothes. They were having a wonderful visit when Mrs. Thomas remarked that she wished she knew what make the dishes were. The doctor, equally curious, wondered whether or not the grapes in the silver epergnes were real, and he said, "Let's find out!" As she turned over a saucer to discover that the china was Lenox, he reached for a grape. It spurted juice all over, for it was real.

The next morning I discovered that my china was Staffordshire and told Mrs. Thomas that she had given me the idea to look. Then she told me that she had found that delightful breakfast set in London, and she added, "I asked Lily to use it for you because I thought you would enjoy it." And I did.

One afternoon we called on Pherbia Thornburg, Lowell's sister, and from her I learned a little about the Thomas ancestry. Her home looks down into the steep valley, her yard still a riot of bloom. The marble-top table in the study was piled high with books with little slips in them for easy reference, so I might browse through them for more to add to these pages—how through sixteen unbroken lines they had been in this country since early Colonial days, mainly English who may have come out of the mountains of Wales when the Romans were in Britain. On his mother's side, partly Dutch of the Peter Stuyvesant period.

On the servants' night out, Frances Thomas drove me into nearby Connecticut along country roads so golden yellow that they seemed to light the way. We dined at an inn that had been a blacksmith shop in the year 1762.

The next day while his lady was at a concert in New York, Mr. Thomas showed me some of his treasures on the top floor of the house, fascinating mementos of various expeditions, pictures, gifts, souvenirs, diplomas from some twenty colleges and universities, most of them honorary doctorates of laws, letters, and the humanities, and books, books, books! In one chest he even had the costumes he had worn in Tibet and in the Arabian desert way back when he was "With Lawrence in Arabia."

He said, "Since Fran is gone, I'd like to have you go down to the dining room for lunch—at noon—and I'll send a car for you at one so that you may sit in on a motion picture episode we are going to do in the studio today for a British broadcasting firm. It all has to do with the story of Lawrence."

At precisely noon I met Henning, the butler, in the doorway of the big dining room. He said, "Mr. Thomas was just in and he wants us to serve you your lunch at the small table over there near the windows. He thought it might be lonely for you to dine at the big table by yourself."

How thoughtful!

At one o'clock a chauffeur came and in a few minutes I was out at the studio conference room where a cheerful fire was blazing on the hearth. A comfortable chair had been placed beside an end table on which were books held in place by pieces of railroad steel, part of a brake shoe from one of the Turkish trains blown up by Lawrence of Arabia on the railroad between Syria and Arabia, between Damascus and Medina.

The room was cluttered with equipment that included a tall crane, camera, cables, and the usual crew, including a director who said to me, "Madame, please do not take notes. This microphone is so delicate it can record even the scratch of a pencil."

Lowell Thomas, in a handsome gray suit, took his place in the chair. All was in readiness.

The director said, "Roll, camera. . . . Action!" and without a note Lowell told the story of Lawrence of Arabia, told it so dramatically and yet so artfully that, although we knew what was coming, we felt the suspense, the excitement and the high adventure of it all.

There was a brief pause while cameras were reloaded and sound adjustments tested. Then again the "Roll, camera. . . . Action" with the narrative continuing.

During the next pause my host grumbled that he knew he could have done better, but the director said, "It was splendid; perfect!"

Another break for the camera to change film and to set up at a different angle. A sudden shout from the director—of anger and disbelief! What in the world had happened? The wood fire had been dying. Someone had put wood on the coals.

At dinner that night I put forth this challenge: "You've seen the whole world, haven't you?"

"No," he said. "I haven't seen the South Pole." That was just before the expedition referred to in an earlier chapter.

"When are you going to see that?" I inquired. My question was purely rhetorical.

"In about two weeks," he replied.

He meant it. Within a short time he was off on another long expedition. But at the time I could not dream that during the year ahead he was to circle the globe three times, visit all continents but South America, and that the Antarctic was to be included twice on his fabulous itinerary. On one of these journeys he flew across the Atlantic to Europe, then from Rome to Portugal, from Lisbon down the west coast of Africa aboard a Pan-Am jet on an inaugural flight to Guinea, the seaport of Conakry, on to Liberia, then south across the equator by way of the Old Ivory and Gold Coasts and Nigeria to the Congo. From Leopoldville, he winged south over the Rhodesias to the Union of South Africa, from where the real adventure began.

Then came what even he was to consider one of the "great flights," an important "aviation first" with Admiral James Reedy and his men—4600 miles nonstop—from Capetown over the empty Antarctic Ocean to the Ultimate South, including a crossing of the Antarctic continent that had never been made before, sights never before seen by man.

After all that adventure the trip home was every bit as dramatic and as hazardous. From McMurdo on the Ross Sea they flew to New Zealand, then on to Australia, making him the first ever to fly from Africa over the Antarctic to Australia—next he did some filming in the aborigine country of Arnhem Land on the Sea of Arafura. After that he headed home by way of Indonesia and Southeast Asia. Pakistan and Afghanistan had been having border troubles, and the usual way of flying from Karachi to the Afghan capital seemed uncertain. So, with Otis Imboden of the National Geographic, he flew to Persia and then from Tehran to Kabul, a central Asian city that he had not visited for over forty years, in the land beyond the Khyber Pass, a then "closed country" which he had been one of the first Americans ever to see.

After a few days in Kabul with his companion, he flew over the lofty Pamirs, across the historic Oxus River and into Russian Central Asia to storied Samarkand. From Turkestan—now called Uzbekistan—the long flight in that Russian plane began, above the Aral Sea and the Kirghiz Steppe, on over the Urals and the Volga, to Moscow.

From the Kremlin he flew out through the Iron Curtain to Scandinavia, then Paris, and home at last.

No one was much surprised when he landed in the Ford Hospital in Detroit after this difficult and wearing journey. Messages poured in from around the world, and here is one of his replies to several "warnings" that he'd best take care of himself. The listeners needed him. I quote:

"They say I've merely had a 'warning.' I suppose there are times when we all need that!

"I have been trying to blame my present visit to Ford Hospital, Detroit, on the Russians, for that was about my last stop on the way home. There is one thing for sure—the Antarctic flight from Africa to the Pole was stimulating, thrilling and inspiring.

"But the time I spent in Arnhem Land, tropical Australia, where the temperatures were around 130 degrees above—may have been the place where a Capricornian bug caught up with me. Anyhow, a couple of days later I had some sort of an attack in Afghanistan. From then on, in Central Asia and in Russia, I took it fairly easy.

"But the other night I was involved in a banquet

where all of the speakers had a bad time because of the acoustics and a hullabaloo going on in an adjoining room. All this went on for four hours, with me as the last speaker. After it was over I knew I was not exactly up to concert pitch, and decided to come in for a checkup.

"This is one of the most impressive hospitals I have ever seen, and Dr. Herman Alvarez and his associates say if I follow their instructions, well, who knows? I might be around for another twenty or thirty years, and able to take part in a dozen more expeditions.

"The doctors say all I have to do is shift from jet to turbo-prop. They say three jaunts around the world, two expeditions to the Antarctic, one to the mountains of New Guinea, another to Central Africa, a journey to the Himalayas to see the Dalai Lama in exile, a trip to central Asia—they think that these journeys added to my usual ski trips to New England, the Rockies, and New Zealand, along with radio, TV and film chores, plus a book, is—well, they think I should slow down. So, I guess I'll have to give up golf!" Yours, L. T.

Within a few days he was back on the air, in time for Thanksgiving, fully recovered and ready to go again. All the world is hopeful that he will be able to go on a dozen or more expeditions and that his usual rugged health will enable him to broadcast for many years to come—AT "CONCERT PITCH."

Herbert Hoover, after one of his many visits to Hammersley Hill, wrote something that probably echoes in many an American's dream. He said, "If I have to have a reincarnation I would prefer it to be Lowell Thomas above all others. It would be an eternal life of adventure, of courage, and of public service."